Product Standards, Exports and Employment

Contributions to Economics

www.springeronline.com/series/1262

Further volumes of this series can be found at our homepage.

Pablo Coto-Millán
General Equilibrium and Welfare
2002. ISBN 7908-1491-1

Wojciech W. Charemza/Krystyna Strzala (Eds.)
East European Transition and EU Enlargement
2002. ISBN 3-7908-1501-1

Natalja von Westernhagen
Systemic Transformation, Trade and Economic Growth
2002. ISBN 3-7908-1521-7

Josef Falkinger
A Theory of Employment in Firms
2002. ISBN 3-7908-1520-9

Engelbert Plassmann
Econometric Modelling of European Money Demand
2003. ISBN 3-7908-1522-5

Reginald Loyen/Erik Buyst/Greta Devos (Eds.)
Struggeling for Leadership: Antwerp-Rotterdam Port Competition between 1870–2000
2003. ISBN 3-7908-1524-1

Pablo Coto-Millán
Utility and Production, 2nd Edition
2003. ISBN 3-7908-1423-7

Emilio Colombo/John Driffill (Eds.)
The Role of Financial Markets in the Transition Process
2003. ISBN 3-7908-0004-X

Guido S. Merzoni
Strategic Delegation in Firms and in the Trade Union
2003. ISBN 3-7908-1432-6

Jan B. Kuné
On Global Aging
2003. ISBN 3-7908-0030-9

Sugata Marjit, Rajat Acharyya
International Trade, Wage Inequality and the Developing Economy
2003. ISBN 3-7908-0031-7

Francesco C. Billari/Alexia Prskawetz (Eds.)
Agent-Based Computational Demography
2003. ISBN 3-7908-1550-0

Georg Bol/Gholamreza Nakhaeizadeh/Svetlozar T. Rachev/Thomas Ridder/Karl-Heinz Vollmer (Eds.)
Credit Risk
2003. ISBN 3-7908-0054-6

Christian Müller
Money Demand in Europe
2003. ISBN 3-7908-0064-3

Cristina Nardi Spiller
The Dynamics of the Price Structure and the Business Cycle
2003. ISBN 3-7908-0063-5

Michael Bräuninger
Public Debt and Endogenous Growth
2003. ISBN 3-7908-0056-1

Brigitte Preissl/Laura Solimene
The Dynamics of Clusters and Innovation
2003. ISBN 3-7908-0077-5

Markus Gangl
Unemployment Dynamics in the United States and West Germany
2003. ISBN 3-7908-1533-0

Pablo Coto-Millán (Ed.)
Essays on Microeconomics and Industrial Organisation, 2nd Edition
2004. ISBN 3-7908-0104-6

Wendelin Schnedler
The Value of Signals in Hidden Action Models
2004. ISBN 3-7908-0173-9

Carsten Schröder
Variable Income Equivalence Scales
2004. ISBN 3-7908-0183-6

Wilhelm J. Meester
Locational Preferences of Entrepreneurs
2004. ISBN 3-7908-0178-X

Russel Cooper/Gary Madden (Eds.)
Frontiers of Broadband, Electronic and Mobile Commerce
2004. ISBN 3-7908-0087-2

Sardar M. N. Islam
Empirical Finance
2004. ISBN 3-7908-1551-9

Jan-Egbert Sturm/Timo Wollmershäuser (Eds.)
Ifo Survey Data in Business Cycle and Monetary Policy Analysis
2005. ISBN 3-7908-0174-7

Bernard Michael Gilroy/Thomas Gries/Willem A. Naudé (Eds.)
Multinational Enterprises, Foreign Direct Investment and Growth in Africa
2005. ISBN 3-7908-0276-X

Günter S. Heiduk/Kar-yiu Wong (Eds.)
WTO and World Trade
2005. ISBN 3-7908-1579-9

Rajat Acharyya

Product Standards, Exports and Employment

An Analytical Study

With 34 Figures and 9 Tables

Physica-Verlag
A Springer Company

Series Editors
Werner A. Müller
Martina Bihn

Author
Dr. Rajat Acharyya
Jadavpur University
Department of Economics
Calcutta 700 032
India
racharya@cal2.vsnl.net.in

ISSN 1431-1933
ISBN 3-7908-1557-8 Physica-Verlag Heidelberg New York

Cataloging-in-Publication Data applied for
Library of Congress Control Number: 2005925716

Physica-Verlag is a part of Springer Science+Business Media

springeronline.com

Printed in Germany

Softcover Design: Erich Kirchner, Heidelberg

SPIN 11019299 88/3153-5 4 3 2 1 0 – Printed on acid-free and non-aging paper

For Joysri, Rajarshi and Ritwik

Preface

Through the process of globalization, the trade dependence and inter-dependence of the developing countries have increased phenomenally than ever before. The characteristic of this late twentieth-century globalization process has been the new technological revolution that has led to a high rate of world exports of electronics and other high-technology products. This has marginalized most of the developing countries exporting largely the low quality and low value-addition manufacturing and primary products, barring a few exceptions like China, India and Mexico. The fruits of globalization have, therefore, been unevenly distributed so far across the developed and the developing countries. Moreover, whatever little growth in exports of medium technology products has been achieved by a few of them, is largely driven by outsourcing of low value-addition and lower-stage of activities by the foreign multinationals. Outsourcing of software services, rather than development of software packages, in India and assembly line for automobiles in Mexico are the two glaring examples. These activities may have boosted the total exports of these countries, but they have failed to generate any feedback effect on the rest of the economy in terms of skill formation, increase in overall productivity level and product diversification.

The possibility of achieving significant export growth by the developing countries has further been constrained by the quality regulations and environmental standards that are often in place on the imports by the advanced industrialized countries. These non-tariff barriers, the new face of protectionism in the twenty-first century, has forced the developing countries to alter their production structures and technology with far reaching implications for the income distribution and the employment opportunities.

These developments reveal a paradox of export-led growth and poverty reduction. To generate strong linkages and dynamic effects with rest of the economy, and to meet the challenges posed by the new set of regulations and standards, the developing countries must enhance their product quality and specialize in high value-addition activities. But this raises the demand for capital, both human and physical, and displaces unskilled labour in the process. As a consequence, not only income inequality may be on the rise, as has already been observed in many parts of the developing world, but increased unemployment among the large number of unskilled workers is also on the card. All these contribute to weaken the positive impact of export growth on poverty alleviation.

This book makes an analytical study of these issues. With the new technological revolution in the West and new set of non-tariff barriers forthcoming on the exports of the developing countries, the export-led development strategy has now quite a different set of requirements and implications than it had ever before. It now requires a good understanding of why developing countries are historically the producers of low-quality and dirty goods and the policy implications thereof. At the same time it is to be understood to what extent changes in the production structures brought about by the quality regulations and environmental standards displace unskilled workers who have almost no alternative employment opportunities. These are the tasks that have been set out in this book.

The basic issues addressed in the book have been drawn heavily from the theoretical work on export quality and income distribution that I started during my visit at the Department of Rochester, New York, as a Ford Foundation Fellow during 1997-98. My recent interest and research in the environmental issues have also shaped much of what has been set out in the book. Some of the research outputs contained in the book have been taught and discussed in special lectures, seminars and informal meetings at the Cornell University (New York), the Michigan State University (East Lansing) and the University of Rochester (New York) in America; the City University of Hong Kong, Hong Kong; the Calcutta University (Kolkata), the Indian Statistical Institute (Kolkata), the Indira Gandhi Institute of Development Research (Mumbai), the Jadavpur University (Kolkata), the Jawaharlal Nehru University (Delhi), the Rabindrabharati University (Kolkata) and the SNDT Women's University (Mumbai) in India; and at the Kobe University in Japan.

My understanding of the issues in international trade, and the general equilibrium and macroeconomic structures that lay the foundation of this book, has been greatly shaped and influenced over the last sixteen years by several teachers, co-authors, friends, colleagues, scholars and, of course, by my students. Among my teachers, I cannot but remember my intellectual debt to Ronald W. Jones, Arup Mallik, Sugata Marjit and Kalyan Sanyal. I have benefited immensely from discussions on the several issues addressed in this book with Sarmila Banerji, Kaushik Basu, Eric Bond, Tarun Kabiraj, Henryk Kierzkowski, Bhaswar Moitra, Mihir Rakshit, Ajitava Raychaudhuri, Prabal Roy Chowdhury, Abhirup Sarkar, Anindya Sen,

Arunava Sen, Kunal Sengupta and Soumen Sikdar. I would also like to thank my students, particularly Swapnendu Bandyopadhyay and Anindita Sen, for cleaning up my ideas through participation in the class lectures and discussions.

Above all, this endeavour owes much to my wife, Joysri, and sons, Rajarshi and Ritwik, as it certainly deprived them of my attention they deserved. They never complained though and had remained as my constant source of inspiration throughout.

March 2005 R. Acharyya

Contents

1 Introduction

With the advent of the new technologies in the late twentieth century that has made possible the production of a commodity in a wide range of varieties and qualities, and with the consumers being aware of such availabilities in the market, competition among firms has taken a new dimension. The price wars have now taken a back seat as an instrument for market invasion and instead differentiation in product characteristics and continuous improvement in quality levels have been the order of the day. Under such circumstances, it is understandable that the poor quality of exports of most of the developing countries, for quite a handful of reasons to be spelled out in later chapters, will be the major impediment for their export growth at the turn of the twentieth century.

With the process of globalization, the tariff barriers are coming down and market access is increasing in most part of the globe. But the poor quality of manufacturing exports of the developing countries in general, is often prohibiting them in exploiting these new opportunities that globalization has generated. As a result, they have been agonizingly marginalized in the new trading environment. Their problem has further been compounded by the non-tariff barriers in the form of quality regulations and environmental standards that are imposed on their exports by an increasing number of advanced industrialized importing countries.

These emerging demand and policy constraints on exports call for a total change in the nature of trade policy in the developing countries. Any sustainable export growth strategy can no longer be aimed at only through the price incentives and cost competitiveness. Product variety and quality now set the pace and magnitude of exports. At the same time they affect, through alteration of production techniques and structures, the distribution of wages and employment across different factors of production. A well thought out long-term trade policy to this end, therefore, should address two sets of issues. First is the cause of poor export quality and the policy impact on the choice of such qualities by the firms. Second, is the implications of the trade policy or the regulation induced quality enhancement on the macroeconomic variables such as income distribution and employment of unskilled workers. This book evolves around these two sets of issues.

1.1 Why Low-Quality Exports?

The developing countries have historically been observed to produce goods of lower quality. Cotton textile industries in the nineteenth-century China and in the late twentieth-century Bangladesh and India have experienced such low-quality phenomena. Even the growth in manufacturing exports in present-day China, Mexico and India has primarily been concentrated in the low-quality and low value-addition activities. Chapter 2 provides an outline of the dimensions of these quality problems.

There are quite a few explanations put forward by economists for the observed poor quality of exports of the developing countries. Essentially higher marginal cost of producing better quality varieties and lack of demand (or lower marginal willingness-to-pay) for these varieties act together to induce the firms in the developing countries to produce lower quality varieties than those produced in the developed industrialized countries. There are also the asymmetric information and reputation problems for the exports of the developing countries.

Backward technologies and slow rates of innovation are the major factors contributing to higher marginal cost. Often protectionist trade policies compound the problem. High tariff on final imports reduce the incentives for innovation, particularly when it requires large investments in R&D and the successful innovation is uncertain [Lall (1984), Acharyya (1995)]. On the other hand, tariff and non-tariff barriers on import of foreign inputs force the domestic exporters to use low quality indigenous inputs. There is also the Heckscher-Ohlin type factor-proportion argument for low quality exports by the developing countries [Acharyya and Jones (2001)]. Since higher quality varieties are usually intensive in physical and/or human capital compared to the lower quality varieties, scarcity of both these factors relative to unskilled labour makes capital-cost higher relative to the wage-cost in the developing countries. This induces the firms to economize on costs by producing lower quality varieties. To enhance product quality, the trade policies should, therefore, be aimed at lowering the capital-cost.

On the other hand, there are two major reasons for lower willingness-to-pay for higher quality. First is the lower income per capita and highly uneven distribution of income in favour of a few rich people in the developing countries. These lead to lower *domestic demand* for higher quality varieties. Second is the asymmetric information of *foreign* buyers in regard to the quality of goods being imported from the developing countries. For goods the quality of which cannot be judged before actual consumption, foreign buyers' marginal willingness-to-pay is influenced by their perceptions about the average industry quality of the goods. Since such perceptions are not very high for goods produced in the developing countries resulting in a lower marginal willingness-to-pay, potentially high-quality producers are discouraged to raise their product quality above the average industry quality. This is similar to Akerlof's (1970) lemon-market story.

In Chapters 3 and 4, I elaborate upon these explanations and trace out the nature of trade and industrial policies that these theories imply to enhance the quality of goods being exported. Another important related issue that is addressed in Chapter 6 is the relationship between skill formation and export quality. It may seem obvious that to the extent higher quality varieties require greater amounts of skilled labour, greater availability of skilled labour through increased skill formation should enhance product quality by lowering the money wage for the skilled workers. What is even more important to note is the reverse causation: To the extent enhanced product quality brings in higher price of exports, the returns to skilled and unskilled workers change and if they change asymmetrically, as has in fact been the case during the process of globalization and trade liberalization in many developing countries, the decision to become skilled is influenced as well. There is thus a two-way causation between the skill formation and the quality level of exports that we should take into account.

1.2 Quality of Exports and Employment

It is understandable that if the importing countries strictly enforce quality regulations and environmental standards and the developing countries fail to live up to the challenge by raising their product standards, the immediate adverse effect would be on employment opportunities. With trade prospects dwindling away, production of exportables will be held back thereby displacing labour. There have already been quite a few cases of labour retrenchment in India as a consequence of shutting down and relocation of production units that failed to meet the minimum environmental standards. It is, however, not yet known how many of them have found alternative employment. In the medium term, some of these displaced workers may be absorbed if production in the rest of the economy increases. But the domestic purchasing power not expanding fast enough to generate any sizeable increase in domestic demand, there will still be a net addition to the pool of unemployed labour force. The problem gets even worse with contraction of import-competing sectors in face of increased and aggressive competition from foreign multinationals. Under such circumstances, enhancement of export quality seems to be the only feasible solution towards employment generation.

There is, however, also the negative side of such quality enhancement. Since higher quality and "cleaner" varieties make less use of unskilled labour than the lower-quality and dirtier varieties, quality enhancement by itself displaces unskilled labour. One should, therefore, weigh this adverse *technique* effect against the favourable *scale* (or foreign-demand) effect in tracing out the net change in aggregate employment of unskilled workers that the quality regulations and environmental standards may result in. A major part of Chapter 5 focuses on these employment aspect of regulations and standards.

The environmental standards trigger some additional employment effects as distinct from the quality regulations. Lower environmental damages inflicted upon the society by the production and consumption of the goods with higher environmental quality improves the productivity of workers and other factors. An improvement in the environmental-quality of the good thus increases the effective supply of the workforce because the same amount of output can now be produced by a smaller amount of labour time. Consequently, if the composition of the output produced in the economy does not change in favour of the relatively labour-intensive goods, such improvements in the environmental-quality of the good can further jeopardize the employment opportunities. Chapter 7 sets out this dimension of the employment effect of the environmental standards.

2 Dimensions of Quality Problem in the Developing Countries

2.1 Low-Quality Phenomenon

Low export quality is a major constraint on the export growth of the developing countries in the advanced industrialized-country markets. This has been well documented by economists and recognized by the policy makers in the developing countries [Rashid (1988), Lall (1984), Acharyya (1995) and Marjit and Raychaudhuri (1997)]. The dimension of poor quality is in fact much wider than just the intrinsic product quality. Packaging and timely delivery are the major part of the problem. Many of the Indian exports suffer from poor packaging leading to breakages, spoilages and consequent return of consignments from the importing countries. During the 1990s, the worst sufferer was the engineering exports accounting for losses in the order of around Rs. 200 crores on an average every year.

There is no direct and comprehensive measure of product quality. This makes any empirical investigation into the nature and extent of the low quality phenomenon and econometric exercise relating export quality and export growth a difficult task. But there are quite a few indirect indicators or yardstick of quality content of export baskets of the developing countries. First of such indirect indicator is the high-technology exports such as chemicals, machines and transport equipments, and scientific instruments like computers, watches, cameras. Second is the ISO 9000 certification for products, which provides a signal to the buyers, particularly who are uncertain about the quality of the product or the reputation of the producers. Of course, these indicators are not complete descriptions of quality characteristics of exports, but a few will disagree that they provide useful starting point.

2.2 High-Technology Exports

The high-technology exports are usually the skill-intensive, quality-differentiated exports. Variations in quality level can be quite large for each of these products depending upon the intensity in which skilled labour is combined with other factors or the level of skill itself of the workforce employed in manufacturing these products. Even among the specialized workforce, for example, skill levels may vary resulting in large variations in the quality levels of the end product. The buyers are also more sensitive to quality variations for these commodities than that for other commodities such as processed primary goods. Thus, the share of the high-technology exports in manufacturing exports of the developing countries may be a first-hand indicator of the quality content of the export basket.

Table 2.1 reports the trends in such shares for a selected group of developing countries of Asia and Latin America. For the selected Latin American countries, except for Brazil after 1999 and for Mexico after 1991, the share of high-technology exports in total manufacturing exports had been well below 10 percent during the 1990s. Argentina in fact had a declining share of high-technology exports.

For the reported Asian countries, on the other hand, except for Korea and China, the shares have been fairly low. Whereas India's share has declined quite steadily from 6.88 percent in 1996, Sri Lanka's export of high-technology goods amounted to little over one percent of its manufacturing exports during the first half of the 1990s.

Table 2.1

High-Technology Exports as a Percentage of Manufacturing Exports

	Latin America				Asia			
	Argentina	Brazil	Mexico	Uruguay	China	India	Korea	Sri Lanka
1991	8.13	5.84	8.60	--	--	4.69	19.41	0.67
1992	8.03	5.88	11.26	--	6.51	4.05	19.81	1.05
1993	6.59	4.39	11.61	2.71	7.20	4.25	20.31	1.13
1994	4.91	5.00	13.93	1.92	8.33	4.79	22.73	1.21
1995	4.10	5.20	15.18	2.63	10.47	5.81	26.07	--
1996	5.67	6.49	15.82	2.66	12.43	6.88	24.11	--
1997	5.13	7.75	17.57	2.19	13.14	6.55	26.69	--
1998	5.96	9.62	19.26	2.11	15.54	5.62	27.14	--
1999	7.66	13.40	20.76	2.43	17.21	--	32.20	3.24
2000	9.04	18.61	22.40	2.13	18.58	5.01	34.82	-
2001	8.96	19.20	22.00	2.13	20.57	5.39	29.55	2.16
2002	7.45	-	21.38	2.87	23.31	4.76	31.52	0.55

Source: World Development Indicator 2004.

However, since there may be a quite large variation in the quality levels of high-technology goods, aggregate value of exports may not always be a satisfactory measure of quality content of export basket. In fact, as Oxfam (2002) observes, many developing countries specialize in the low-quality varieties of these goods. For example, Mexico is the second largest exporter of medium-technology manufacturing goods in the world after Korea and ahead of Taiwan and sixth largest exporter of high-technology goods. Yet it typifies a pattern of low-quality exports of these items.

Thus what seem to be more appropriate are the destinations to which such exports are made. Given the fact that buyers in the industrialized countries are relatively more quality conscious than buyers in the developing countries, precisely because of the differences in their preference pattern due to income differences, high-technology exports in the industrialized-country markets relative to those in the other developing-country markets may be a better indicator of the quality content. For example, most of the exports of engineering goods of India, which is among its five top export goods, are destined to the market in UAE. Similar logic applies to other exports as well.

Table 2.2 shows share of the European Union (EU) market in India's total exports and India's share in EU's extra-EU total imports. Whereas the former had declined steadily throughout the first half of the 1990s, India's market share in the EU (column 3) increased only marginally from 0.91 percent in 1991 to 1.14 percent in 1996.

Table 2.2
India's Exports to EU in the 1990s

	EU's Share in Total Exports of India	India's Share in EU's Extra-EU Imports
1991	29.43	0.91
1992	29.57	1.07
1993	27.13	1.18
1994	27.86	1.16
1995	27.47	1.19
1996	25.95	1.14

Source: Acharyya and Raychaudhuri (2001).

Figure 2.1: Share of Exports to USA in Total Exports of India, Sri Lanka, Korea and China

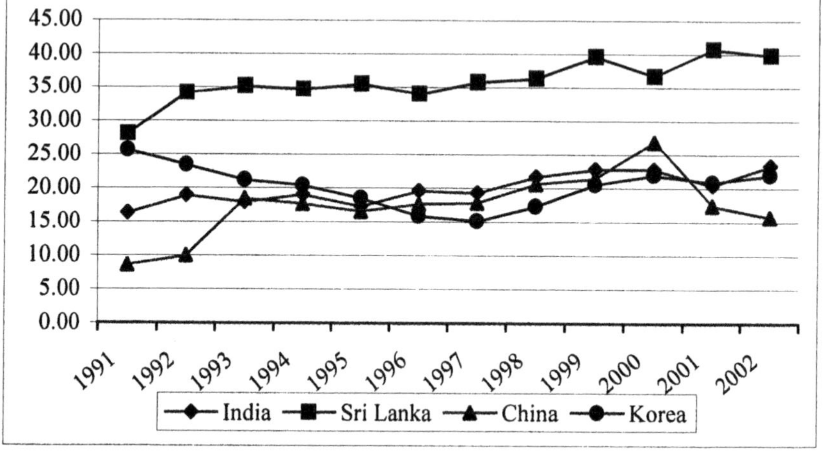

Source: UNCTAD Commodity Trade Statistics.

Note that this is the period when large price incentives were provided to the Indian exporters through large devaluation and liberalization of the exchange rate and through liberalization of import regime including import of capital goods. Despite of such incentives, part of the reason why exports in the EU markets could not be raised to any significant extent must be related to the poor export quality.

Figure 2.1, on the other hand, depicts the trends in share of exports of India, Sri Lanka, China and Korea to the US market in their respective aggregate exports during 1991-2002. After 1993, such shares for India, China and Korea have moved more or less together around the 20 percent level. Thus, USA has been the major destination of exports for all these countries. The dependence of Sri Lanka on the US market for its exports is even higher.

But when we look at the market share that these countries command in USA during the same period, the differences in competitiveness of exports of these countries is immediately evident. Whereas share of India in total imports of USA had touched one percent only in 2002, that of Sri Lanka had remained well below one percent (see Figure 2.2). China's share, on the other hand, increased from one percent in 1991 to five percent in 2002. At the beginning of the 1990s, Korea had such a high share as China has achieved in 2001, but its importance as a source of US imports has declined since then. Still, Korea commands a market share of little less than 3 percent in 2002. Apart from standard cost competitiveness of exports, which may have established comparative advantages of China and Korea in many export items vis-à-vis Indian and Sri Lankan exports, differences in quality of such exports across these countries also must have accounted for these differences in market shares.

Of course, one might argue that high tariff and non-tariff barriers in the industrialized countries against the imports from the developing countries, rather than the quality content, should be a major constraining factor and thus provides an explanation of slow growth of exports in these markets. But what should in fact matter in this context are the trade barriers in these countries relative to that in the developing countries. While trade barriers on agricultural products are certainly higher in the developed countries, the situation is altogether different for manufacturing goods. The developing country tariffs on manufacturing imports are almost three times higher than tariffs imposed by the industrialized countries on similar exports from the developing countries.

Figure 2.2: Share of India, Sri Lanka, Korea and China in Total Import of USA

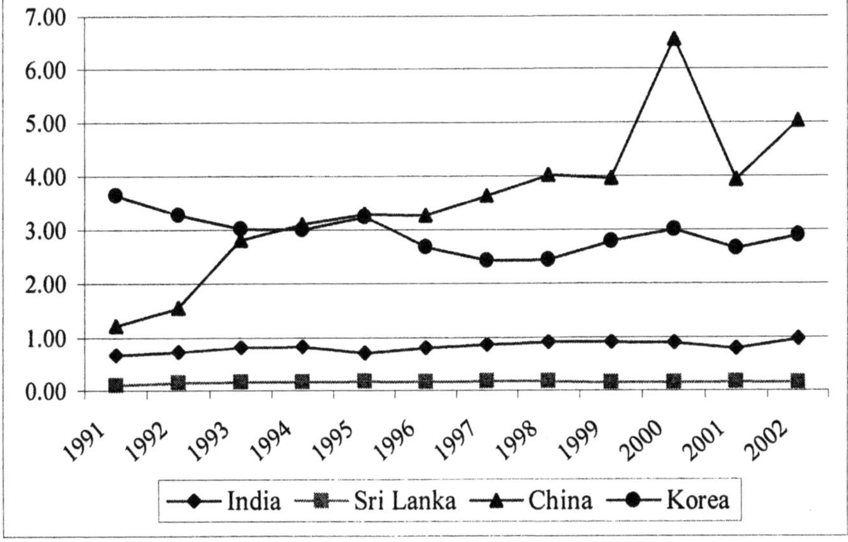

Source: UNCTAD Commodity Trade Statistics.

Table 2.3 reflects upon such a possible quality-constraint on Indian exports at the disaggregate level. Shares of India and China in total import of machinery and transport equipment, a major component of high-technology exports, by the European countries, the USA and Canada, indicate the quality difference of these products exported by China and India. The shares of the EU and the US together in exports of both China and India were between 35 and 40 percent during 1995-1998. But the shares of India in these markets had been rather insignificant. Thus, though the European and the US markets were principal destinations of Indian exports of machines and transport equipment, together accounting for almost 40 percent, India was not a major source of supply for their imports.

Table 2.3

Exports of Machines and Transport Equipment of China and India

	Share in India's Total Export of Machines				India's Share in Total Import of Machines			
	1995	1996	1997	1998	1995	1996	1997	1998
BENELUX	2.74	3.50	2.99	3.08	0.09	0.12	0.10	0.08
Germany	4.72	4.03	5.07	6.65	0.07	0.07	0.09	0.09
France	1.38	1.08	1.59	2.12	0.03	0.03	0.05	0.04
UK	7.76	8.26	6.12	6.39	0.17	0.19	0.13	0.11
EU-15	22.99	22.86	22.08	26.95	0.09	0.09	0.09	0.08
USA	12.68	18.83	16.00	14.44	0.08	0.14	0.11	0.08
Canada	0.43	0.59	0.77	0.80	0.01	0.02	0.02	0.02
Japan	0.85	0.94	1.44	2.76	0.03	0.03	0.05	0.09
	Share in China's Total Export of Machines				**China's Share in Total Import of Machines**			
	1995	1996	1997	1998	1995	1996	1997	1998
BENELUX	2.83	3.65	4.43	5.11	0.96	1.28	1.78	2.21
France	1.32	1.31	1.56	1.91	0.43	0.46	0.70	0.86
Germany	4.58	4.53	4.41	4.94	0.92	1.01	1.25	1.46
UK	2.32	2.67	2.81	3.33	0.67	0.78	0.92	1.19
EU 15	13.41	14.37	15.76	18.59	0.65	0.73	0.97	1.19
USA	19.72	20.22	20.93	23.44	1.73	1.93	2.27	2.73
Canada	0.87	1.20	1.07	0.88	2.05	2.94	2.91	2.61
Japan	13.96	15.27	14.01	12.92	5.77	6.33	7.32	8.67

Source: PC-TAS 2000 CD-ROM (UNCTAD Commodity Trade database).

China, on the other hand, though managed a share of over 1 percent only in 1998 in the European markets, fared quite well in the North American markets and in Japan. In fact, despite decline in her dependence on Japan as a market for these exports, China has been able to increase its market share in Japan quite consistently. This indicates growing importance of China as a source of import of machines and transport equipment by Japan. Quality factor, apart from standard cost competitiveness of Chinese exports, might have been an important factor underlying this.

There is, however, one major problem with such destination criterion of high quality exports. High technology exports to industrialized-country markets may essentially be locally low value added activities. The glaring example of all is the automobile exports of Mexico to the US. By the turn of the twenty-first century, Mexico has emerged as the single largest supplier of engines and passenger vehicles in the US due to relocation of assembling units of Ford, General Motors and Chrysler in Mexico. But these assembling units generate only about one-tenth of the value added in Mexico's manufacturing sector [Oxfam (2002)]. Thus the strength of dynamic links between exports and the domestic economy should be a proper yardstick of export quality. What one should perhaps look at is whether export activities involve high local value addition.

On this count too many developing countries fare quite badly. In Philippines, electronics account for over 80 percent of exports, but these have been driven almost entirely by the semi-conductor assembly [Lall (2001)]. The phenomenal growth of the Indian software industry in the 1990s, on the other hand, has been due to outsourcing of low value addition activities by the foreign multinationals. As Basu (2001) observes, Indian software exports have been dominated by export of software services rather than software packages. Indian firms primarily focus on custom computer programming, manpower training, and consultation. In 1990 the share of service in total software exports was 90 percent, which increased to 97 percent in the year 2000. In contrast, some of her competitors have relied less heavily on export of software service and have been able to develop and export software packages as well (see Table 2.4).

2.3 ISO Series Certification

The ISO series standards are well recognized Quality Management System developed by the International Standards Organization in Geneva in 1987.

The first revision of this system was done in 1994 and the second in the year 2000. The ISO-9001 series certification, that is applicable to contractual situations, is based on eight quality management principles among which customer focused organization, process approach and scope of continual improvement are particularly relevant in the context of quality of product.

Table 2.4

Composition of Software Exports in 1990

	Service	Package	Data Entry
India	90	5	5
China	17	56	27
Israel	19	76	5
Mexico	53	32	15
Philippines	39	20	41
Singapore	25	58	17

Source: As reported in Heeks (1996).

The ISO-9004 series, on the other hand, are applicable in non-contractual situations. The concept of quality is not just defined with respect to the product standard, but also in relation to marketing, supply and services. As such though these certifications may not always indicate the actual quality-content of the product itself, they create overall perceptions about the company or the brand name and thereby influence the buyers' willingness-to-pay for such products. As we will see later in Chapter 3, when buyers are not well informed about products they buy or the nature of the product is such that it is not possible to judge its quality before consumption, the so called experience goods generating informational externality [Akerlof (1970)], ISO-9000 certificate can be an indicator of high quality. Thus, with comparable prices, buyers would like to buy brands with ISO-9000 label than brands without such label. Their willingness-to-pay for the product is also expected to vary with such labeling. In fact, quite a few industrialized countries are now imposing such requirements on imports from the developing countries. As observed by Sharma et.al. (1997), in 1993 India had problems in obtaining ISO-9000 certificates from the European agencies for its export of instruments and electronics, which adversely affected such exports to the European Union. There is also some positive cross-country empirical relationship found by Raychaudhuri et. al. (2002) between the number of companies having ISO-9000 certificate and aggregate exports of countries.

Table 2.5 shows the growth of the number of ISO-certified companies in selected developing countries relative to that in the United Kingdom and the US. Except in China and Korea during 1999-2000, growth of such companies in these developing countries has been far below that in the United Kingdom and the US. Bangladesh and Sri Lanka have been the worst performers in this respect. Among the Latin American countries, only in Brazil in the late 1990s, growth of such companies has picked up, similar to what can be observed for India. But overall performances of the Latin American countries are even worse than the African and South Asian countries.

Table 2.5

Cumulative Number of ISO Companies in Selected Countries

	1993	1995	1997	1999	2000
Argentina	9	86	397	1388	2056
Bangladesh			1	25	25
Brazil	113	923	2068	6257	6719
China	35	507	5698	15109	25657
India	73	1023	2865	5200	5682
Korea	87	619	5806	11533	15424
Malaysia	224	690	1610	1921	2355
Mexico	24	215	711	1556	1843
Sri Lanka	1	7	38	82	82
Thailand	9	143	1104	1527	2553
UK	28096	52595	56696	63700	63725
USA	2059	8762	18581	33054	35018
Share of Africa & South Asia	2.64	2.65	3.88	5.04	4.94
Share of Central & Latin America	0.68	0.96	1.34	2.61	2.64

Note: Figures for the year 1993 are till September. For rest of the years the numbers indicate ISO companies at the end of December.

Source: ISO 9000 CD-ROM.

This is evident from the share of Africa and South Asia, and of Central and Latin America in total number of ISO companies in the world shown in the last two rows. However, what is to be noted is that not all of these companies are exporters. That is, the number of export companies having ISO-9000 series certificate is even less than the numbers shown in Table 2.5.

As I shall argue later, the absolute numbers or the share of companies or regions in the world aggregate of ISO companies may not be a good measure of average industry quality for reasons well spelled out in theory. Rather, the more relevant and accurate reflector would be the proportion of the ISO-9000 companies in an industry.

Table 2.6
Ratios of ISO to Non-ISO Companies and Exports to Sales for Selected Indian Industries in 1999-2000

Industry	ISO/non-ISO Firms	Export/Sales
Food & Beverages	0.19	10.61
Tea & Coffee	0.22	22.72
Poultry & Meat Products	0.16	49.49
Cotton Textiles	0.12	26.55
Readymade Garments	0.39	53.04
Chemicals	0.11	4.12
Drugs & Pharmaceuticals	0.16	18.55
Gems & Jeweler	0.45	88.05
Electronics	0.44	22.71
Computer Software	0.34	46.56
Footwear	0.42	32.25

Source: CMIE, 2001; Q-prod.com.

Table 2.6 reports the percentage of the ISO companies in some of the Indian industries and the export share in total sales of these industries. Industries like gems and jeweler, electronics, computer software, readymade garments and footwear have quite high percentage of ISO-9000 companies. Except the electronics sector, the export performance of these industries relative to the domestic sales have also been quite good.

The positive correlation between the ratio of ISO to non-ISO firms and ratio of exports to total sales across these industries has also been reasonably high at the statistically significant level of 0.58. Raychaudhuri et. al. (2003) also observe a statistically significant high value of rank correlation at 0.72 between sectoral distribution of ISO companies and aggregate exports for the Indian industries in the year 2000.

2.4 Dirty Exports and Environmental Standards

Another aspect of product quality is the environmental damages that a product causes either when it is produced or when it is consumed. Industrial activities and cigarette smoking are the two examples of such production and consumption pollutions respectively. However, the degree or magnitude of the environmental damages may differ from one good to another. Similarly, different varieties (or qualities) of the same good may have different degrees of pollution emission. The goods (or varieties) which inflict upon higher environmental damages than others, are called the dirty goods (or varieties) in contrast to the clean good or cleaner varieties. Manufacturing goods like iron & steel, metal manufactures, ferrous and non-ferrous metals, refined petroleum and paper manufacture have high pollution content and accordingly are labeled as the dirty goods. Historically, at least till the 1980s, the industrialized countries of the West were the major producers and exporters of these goods. Countries like Australia, Germany, Canada, France and UK, not only had a very high share of these goods in their respective total exports, but also had a very high share of world trade in these items [Low and Yeats (1992)]. Germany had almost 12 percent of world trade in dirty goods whereas the USA and Canada had 7.4 percent and 6.6 percent shares respectively in 1988. The situation, however, has changed dramatically from the early 1990s as the concerns for protecting the national as well as global environment increased.

With the late industrialization process, the composition of output has, on the other hand, changed significantly towards the dirty goods in the developing countries. Consequently, they have now become major exporters of such goods.

Figure 2.3 shows the growth of exports of dirty goods by some of the developing and developed countries during 1990s. Except for Argentina and South Africa, for all these countries the share of dirty goods in five categories – metal mining, nonferrous metals, pulp and paper, iron and steel, and chemicals -- taken together in country exports has fallen during this period. Both China and India have kept exports of these highly polluting goods at less than 10 percent of their aggregate exports. These shares are comparable to those of the USA and Japan. But such goods assume still quite high proportions of exports for Australia, Germany and Canada.

But, in terms of volume and value of exports of dirty goods, some of the developed countries still remain as the major exporters. For example, though USA and Japan have similar shares of dirty exports in their respective total exports as India and China have, absolute value of their exports is much higher. For example, in 1999, dirty exports of USA were more than 300 percent higher than that of China and more than 1700 percent higher than that of India. Japan, on the other hand, exported dirty goods by more than 200 percent higher than did China. Understandably, the world shares of dirty exports for USA and Japan are significantly higher than those for China and India. To the extent to which environmental degradation depends positively with the volume of exports, these have far reaching implications.

Figure 2.3: Growth of Dirty Exports in 1990s

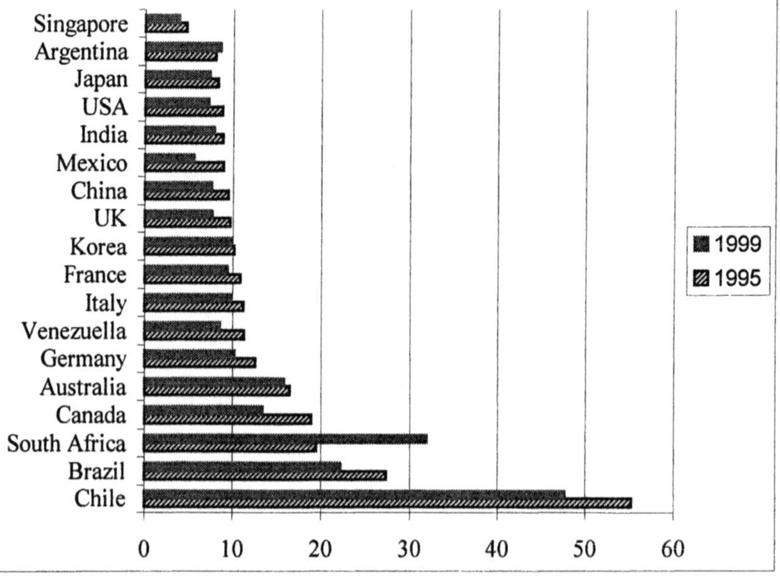

However, quite a large number of firms in these countries have also adopted cleaner technologies for producing the dirty goods thereby reducing the environmental damages despite of large-scale production (Table 2.7). This is evident from the many-fold increase in the number of firms having ISO-14000 series certificate during 1995-2000. Performances of the firms in the developing countries in this regard, except in Korea and China, have remained quite poor. Once again, though meaningful conclusions can be drawn only on the basis of information regarding what proportions of national firms have adopted cleaner technologies, growth in absolute numbers of ISO-14000 firms indicate at least the asymmetry in the extent of adoption of cleaner technologies. Situation is certainly worst in high-polluting countries like South Africa and Venezuela.

Table 2.7

Adoption of Cleaner Technology: ISO 14000 Firms

	1995	1998	2000
Argentina	1	37	114
Australia	1	352	1049
Brazil	2	88	330
Canada		104	475
China		94	510
France	3	295	710
Germany	35	651	1260
India	1	40	257
Italy		123	521
Japan	4	1542	5556
Korea	19	263	544
Mexico		39	159
Singapore		78	100
South Africa		30	126
UK	61	921	2534
USA	1	291	1042
Venezuela		1	7

Source: ISO 10th Cycle Survey.

It has also been observed that in many developing countries lax environmental standards have further encouraged capital flight and relocation of production of dirty goods from the developed countries.

Sometimes, the standards are deliberately kept low by the local governments to attract such multinational activities. Table 2.8 below, reproduced from Wilson et. al. (2002), reports cross-country index of stringency in environmental regulation developed by Dasgupta et. al. (2001) on the basis of their survey on the scope and enforcement of legislation enacted to protect natural resources like air, water and land[1]. A higher score in their index means more stringent environmental standards. Except Korea, the Asian and Latin American countries reported here have very lax environmental regulations. Brazil, China and India, on the other hand, appear to be countries with moderately stringent environmental standards.

Table 2.8

Stringency of Environmental Regulation: Dasgupta et. al (2001) Index

Maximum Score = 24

Stringent		Moderate		Lax	
Germany	24	South Africa	19	Kenya	12
Ireland	24	China	17	Philippines	12
Netherlands	24	India	16	Zambia	12
Switzerland	24	Brazil	14	Thailand	10
Bulgaria	23			Bangladesh	9
Korea	22			Paraguay	9
Finland	21				

Source: Compiled from Wilson et. al. (2002)

This has in fact become the bone of contention between the developed and the developing countries. The developed countries complain about the unfair trade that the developing countries are engaged in as a consequence of comparative advantage in dirty goods gained through lax environmental standards and consequently regulate such imports from the developing countries. On the other hand, the reaction in the developing countries

[1] Using the UNCTAD survey in 1976, Tobey (1990) measured environmental stringency on a scale of one to seven. Another available measure is that of Levinson (1996) who used six different measures of environmental stringency.

against such environmental regulations has been quite strong as they view these policy measures as new protectionism.

However, environmental regulations have some static welfare implications as well for both the developed and the developing countries. To the extent to which environmental regulations imposed by the developed countries on exports by developing countries, requiring cleaner technologies to be adopted for production, raise cost of production, not only exports become less competitive but also cost more to the consumers in the developed countries. Given such considerations, as we will see later, environmental taxes and regulations on Southern exports, which are certainly not the first-best policy option, may even be worse than the free trade policy for the developed or the Northern countries.

2.5 Conclusion

Quality problems in the developing countries have many dimensions ranging from low intrinsic quality and high pollution-content of the good to low-quality packaging, delivery and servicing. These seriously constrain the export growth of the developing countries. On the other hand, in a few cases where the low and medium quality exports have grown to some extent, such as in case of China and Mexico, such growth have failed to generate any productivity increase in the rest-of-the-economy. That is, such exports have not contributed to overall increase in productive capacity.

One should, therefore, understand the underlying causes of such low-quality phenomena and design the trade and industrial policies accordingly to push the economy towards a long-term and sustainable export growth path. Following chapters examines such causes and policies.

3 Theories of Quality Choice

3.1 Introduction

There are quite a handful of theoretical explanations for the low-quality phenomena in the developing countries. In this chapter we look at these theories and examine how they can shed lights on the Indian and developing country experiences.

I begin with the discussion of the factors that influence the choice of product quality by firms. Then I address how the heterogeneity among the consumers might induce firms to offer them more than one quality or variety of the product. The starting point of these analyses is the pioneering works of Mussa and Rosen (1978) and Gabszweicz and Thisse (1979), that focus on firms and the vertically differentiated industry under consideration rather than on the economy as a whole. But these micro-foundations are important to understand as most of the general equilibrium treatment that follow this chapter will be built around them.

In Section 3.3, I elaborate upon how these basic theories can be applied to explain differences in the export qualities across countries. Section 3.4 discusses some of the alternative explanations towards the low-quality phenomenon in the developing countries. In this context, we draw out the implications of ISO-9000 certifications.

3.2 Choice of Product Quality by Firms

The choice of product qualities by a single firm and a perfectly competitive industry was first analyzed independently by Mussa and Rosen (1978) and Gabszweicz and Thisse (1979). The subsequent literature that grew out of these two seminal works has involved itself in quite a few diversified sets of issues. The basic premise underlying all these analyses, however, is that the consumers' utility, both marginal and total, varies positively with the quality level that can be observed by them. Accordingly, consumers are willing to pay a higher price, for any *given* quantity that they buy, if quality of the product is higher than they would if it is lower. This provides the incentive for the firms to raise quality of the product. Of course, if quality of a product can be raised without much addition to total cost (or in a costless way), the product quality offered at equilibrium would have been the topmost quality permissible by the existing set of technology.

What appears is that the marginal willingness-to-pay and the cost of quality are the two basic forces underlying the choice of product quality. Since tastes and incomes determine the marginal willingness-to-pay for quality, these two constitute the demand factors that influence the quality choice. Much of the observed differences in product qualities across countries can thus be traced down to these factors along with the technological asymmetry that provides us the supply-side explanation.

Does the market structure play any role? As Mussa and Rosen (1978) demonstrate, it does. With firms catering different qualities to the heterogeneous set of consumers having different marginal willingness-to-pay, they show that a monopolist will offer lower qualities than the perfectly competitive firms.

Of course, the implicit assumption that we have made so far is that the consumers can observe the true product qualities. There is thus no asymmetry in information across the producers and the consumers. This is the case for a wide range of products, which Nelson (1974) called *search goods*. At the same time, there are the *experience goods* for which product quality can be judged only after the purchase and consumption. Under such circumstances buyers' marginal willingness-to-pay, that in turn determines the choice of true quality of the product, is based on their *perception* about the average industry quality. Accordingly, as amply demonstrated by Chiang and Masson (1988), market concentration rather than competition raises product quality through its favourable influence on the average industry quality. Thus, the implication of the market structure on the product quality choice can be significantly different for experience goods.

The role of demand factors, technology and market structure in determining the choice of quality for search goods can be illustrated with the help of the following simple structure. Consider a set of consumers N, consuming only one unit each of a vertically differentiated good. The quality of the good indexed by $q \in [0, \bar{q}]$ is observable to all. This range of possible qualities is determined by the state of the existing technology. At present, suppose all consumers are identical in their tastes and in their incomes. This amounts to identical marginal willingness-to-pay for all. The utility of a representative consumer is strictly increasing in the quality level of the good and thus when confronted with same price, he strictly prefers the higher quality to the lower quality. Formally, the utility function is specified as,

$$U = u(\alpha, q) \tag{3.1}$$

with the following restrictions :

$$u(\alpha,0) > 0, u_q(\alpha,q) > 0, u_{qq}(\alpha,q) \leq 0 \tag{3.2}$$

where, α denotes the type of the consumer which may be the taste or the income level. Since all consumers are assumed to identical, the value of α is same for all. The signs in (3.2) indicate that the utility increases with the quality (i.e., the marginal utility from quality in strictly positive) but at a non-decreasing rate. These are fairly standard restrictions.

However, a representative consumer participates in the market (i.e., buys the good) only if he gets strictly non-negative *net* utility:

$$V = u(\alpha, q) - p \geq 0 \tag{3.3}$$

where, p is the price that he pays[2]. The strict equality, $V = 0$, defines what is called market-participation or individual rationality constraint. This is shown in Figure 1. It states that for any given quality (q) and type (α), what should be the maximum price that will induce the consumer to participate in the market and accept that price-quality menu. Any price lower than this maximum price will leave the consumer with strictly positive net utility for that quality level and hence will make him better off. This is captured through the successively lower iso-net-utility curves or indifference curves between price and quality. In other words, the curve $a'a'$ (or $a''a''$) represents the different price-quality menu for which the consumer gets the same but strictly positive net utility. Thus the consumer remains indifferent between all such menus. Note that the particular slope and shape of the indifferent curves follow from (3.2) because given (3.3), the marginal utility from quality equals the marginal rate of substitution between price and quality.

Let us now turn to the producers' selection of a price-quality menu given such a preference pattern that implies an increasing marginal willingness-to-pay for quality. Since the consumers are alike, the assumed preference

[2] In the literature the constant marginal utility of income is normalized to unity so that p measures the utility foregone by paying the price for one unit.

structure together with the market participation constraint imply that total demand for any price-quality menu is either zero or N:

$$D = \begin{cases} N & \text{if } V \geq 0 \\ 0 & \text{otherwise} \end{cases} \tag{3.4}$$

Suppose, the marginal cost of production for any given quality is constant, but increasing at an increasing rate with the quality enhancement:

$$C = c(q)x,\ c(0) > 0,\ c_q(q) > 0,\ c_{qq}(q) > 0 \tag{3.5}$$

where, x is the output of a representative firm which equals either zero or N. Thus, we assume diminishing returns of the productive services with respect to quality of the product.

In a competitive market, profits are driven down to zero as the price equals the marginal cost of production:

$$p = c(q) \tag{3.6}$$

On top of this we have the marginal-quality condition that requires equality between the marginal willingness-to-pay for quality and the marginal cost of quality on the basis of which producers select the product quality:

$$u_q(\alpha, q) = c_q(q) \tag{3.7}$$

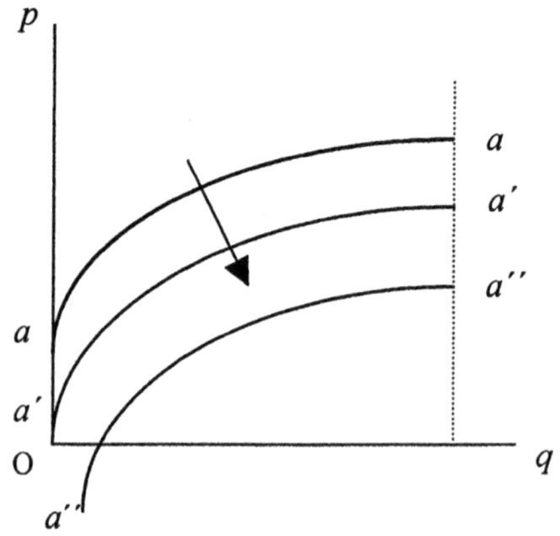

Figure 3.1: Preference Structure

Such a competitive price-quality menu (p_C, q_C) is shown in Figure 3.2 for a representative consumer.

Few comments are warranted at this point. First, we assume $c(q) < u(\alpha, 0)$ so that even for very low quality levels there exists at least one price that covers the marginal cost and yet induces the consumer to participate in the market. Second, to ensure an interior solution (i.e., $q_C < \bar{q}$) we must put following restrictions on the curvature property of the cost and preference functions:

$$c_q(\bar{q}) > u_q(\alpha, \bar{q}) \tag{3.8}$$

Given (3.2) and (3.5), this ensures that the marginal quality condition holds for some quality level strictly lower than the topmost feasible quality[3]. It is immediate that the competitive quality depends on the marginal cost of quality and the marginal willingness-to-pay. An increase in marginal cost should therefore lower the competitive quality whereas an increase in marginal willingness-to-pay should enhance it.

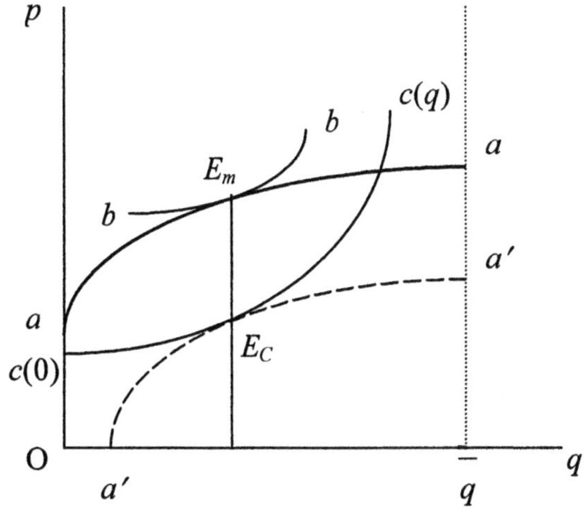

Figure 3.2: Competitive and Monopoly Qualities

[3] This has been demonstrated in Acharyya (1998). On the other hand, strict convexity of the cost function and concavity of the preference function imply uniqueness of such a solution, if exists.

How a monopolist would have chosen the price-quality menu? His problem is to maximize,

$$\pi = [p - c(q)]x \tag{3.9}$$

subject to the individual rationality constraint (3.3). The monopoly equilibrium for a representative consumer in Figure 3.1 is the point of tangency E_m between the individual rationality constraint locus and the highest possible (unit) iso-profit curve. The (unit) iso-profit curve such as bb represents the price-quality combination that yields the same level of profit for the monopolist by selling one unit of the good to a representative consumer.

What is to be noted is that the monopolist offers the same quality as the competitive firms (or, as matter of fact, what a social planner would have offered). This follows from the fact that the (unit) iso-profit curves have the same curvature property as the cost curve,

$$\left.\frac{dq}{dp}\right|_{\pi} = c_q(q) \ \forall\ q$$

whereas the preference function defined in (3.3) is such that the indifference curves are *vertically parallel.*

Therefore, there would be no quality distortion under monopoly but only the price would be raised above the marginal cost of production to extract all the surplus from the consumers. That is, the monopolist will push them to their reservation (net) utility. However, total surplus would still be the same simply because the consumers' surplus at the competitive (or social welfare maximizing) solution would be merely transferred to the monopolist.

This particular result follows from two typical feature of the standard model. First is what we have pointed out above, the same level of quality is chosen by the monopolist as well as by the competitive firms. Second is due to the assumption that consumers buy, if at all, only one unit of the good. There is, however, one case where even with these assumptions, quality distortion arises under market imperfection. This is the case when more than one quality is offered at equilibrium. Of course, this necessitates the existence of a heterogeneous set of consumers who have either different tastes or different income levels such that their marginal willingness-to-pay differs. Note that with all buyers alike, i.e., having the same marginal willingness-to-pay for quality, there would be only one quality offered as illustrated above.

Suppose that there are two types of consumers: n_1 number of type-α_1 consumers and n_2 number of type-α_2 consumers. Let $\alpha_2 > \alpha_1$. Thus, α_2 consumers are the high-taste consumers. Of course, we could have considered a continuum of types with α defined over some closed interval $[\alpha, \bar{\alpha}]$ as in Mussa and Rosen (1978). However, the discrete case, with only two types, drives home our point without any loss of generality[4]. With such heterogeneous set of consumers, the literature usually puts following set of restrictions on the preference structure of the different types. For $\alpha_2 > \alpha_1$ and all $q \in [0, \bar{q}]$,

$$u(\alpha_2, q) > u(\alpha_1, q) \qquad (3.10a)$$

$$u_q(\alpha_2, q) > u_q(\alpha_1, q) \qquad (3.10b)$$

That is, the high-type consumers derive both greater total and marginal utility than the low-type for any given quality of the product. The individual rationality constraint of the high-type thus lies wholly above that of the low-type and the indifference curves of the two types cut each other. However, since (3.10b) is assumed to hold for all possible quality levels, the indifference curves cross only once indicating unique ranking of the marginal willingness-to-pay of the respective types[5].

The difference in the marginal willingness-to-pay of the different types is absolutely critical for the possibility that the market offers two separate qualities, though it may not be a sufficient condition. For example, suppose $u_q(\alpha_2, q) = u_q(\alpha_1, q)$. That is, even though the high-type consumers derive strictly greater total utility, they derive the same marginal utility as the low-type. In such a situation the marginal willingness-to-pay of the two types would also be the same and accordingly the firms would have no incentive to provide different qualities to them. Thus, assumption (3.10b) is important in explaining coexistence of different varieties or qualities in the market.

---

[4] See Acharyya (1998) and Cooper (1984) for the discrete model we consider here.
[5] This single-crossing property is critical in the models of self-selection like this. See Cooper (1984).

With different marginal willingness-to-pay across the different types generating scope for such quality differentiation by the firms, the individual rationality (IR) constraint for the two types like (3.3) alone cannot specify the demand structure. Consumers must now also decide about which quality to buy, i.e., which price-quality configuration among the two to accept, once they decide to participate in the market. This choice in fact, determines the market for each variety or quality. Consider any two qualities, $q_2 > q_1$ and corresponding prices $p_2 > p_1$, that satisfy the IR constraint of the type-α_j consumers. Then a representative type-α_j consumer will buy the higher quality product (at a higher price, of course) if he derives at least the same net utility that he can enjoy from buying the lower quality product. That is, he accepts (p_2, q_2) if,

$$u(\alpha_j, q_2) - p_2 \geq u(\alpha_j, q_1) - p_1, j = 1,2 \tag{3.11}$$

This is the self-selection (SS) or the incentive compatibility constraint. In case of strict equality in (3.11), the tie-breaking rule is that the consumer purchases the higher quality product. Given such preference patterns of the high and the low types, the equilibrium qualities offered by a representative competitive firm and a monopolist are illustrated in Figure 3.3. The marginal quality conditions for the two types of consumers, $c_q(q_j) = u_q(\alpha_j, q_j)$ determines the two competitive qualities. These correspond to the points of tangencies, e_1 and e_2, between the cost curve and the indifference curves $a_1'a_1'$ and $a_2'a_2'$ respectively for the low and the high type. Thus the high type is offered a higher quality (at a higher price, of course) than the quality offered to the low type.

Note that for such a price-quality menu, $(p_2 = e_2 q_{2C}, q_{2C})$, the high-type consumers derive strictly greater net utility than if they would select the menu $(e_1 q_{1C}, q_{1C})$ that is offered to the low-type consumers. This is evident from the fact that the indifference curve for the high type that passes through point e_1 lies above $a_2'a_2'$ indicating lower net utility for them. That is the SS constraint (3.11) is satisfied as strict inequality so that the high-type will indeed buy the higher quality product targeted at them. Similarly since $a_1'a_1'$ lies below the indifference curve for the low-type that passes through e_2, the low-type consumers derive greater net utility by consuming the lower quality product at a lower price. Hence we have a self-selecting separating equilibrium where neither type has any incentive to mimic the other. By choosing the menu targeted at them, they reveal their true types.

Does a monopolist provide the same qualities? Of course not. Whereas the high-type consumers will be offered the same quality, the low-type consumers will get a lower quality. Thus there will be quality distortion at the low-end of the market. In the continuum of type case, Mussa and Rosen (1978) demonstrated that except at the high-end of the market, everywhere else there would be quality distortion in the sense that all those qualities would be degraded by the monopolist[6]. In fact, depending upon the distribution pattern, as established earlier [White (1977), Donnenfeld and White (1988) and Acharyya (1998)], the monopolist may cater only to the high-type by offering q_{2C}. That is, the incentive for the monopolist to degrade the quality offered to the low-type increases with the increase in the relative size of the high-type consumers and in some cases it may be so strong that he degrades quality to the maximum and virtually does not cater to the low-type consumers.

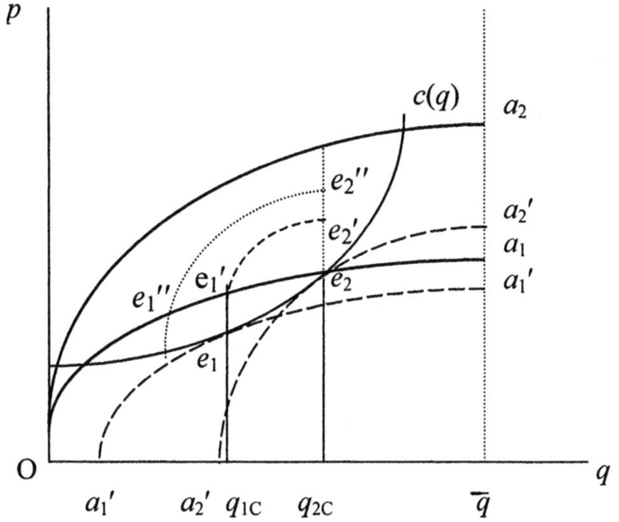

Figure 3.3: Quality Differentiation

To explain all these, note that if the monopolist caters to the low-type consumers at all, he extracts their entire surplus by charging a price for any quality so as to push them to their reservation net utility. Thus a

[6] This result had later been reiterated in Besanko, Donnenfeld and White (1988) and Donnenfeld and White (1988).

representative low-type consumer will always be offered a menu along his IR constraint. The high-type will then be offered a menu, a higher quality product at a higher price, which should fetch him exactly the same net utility as he gets from selecting the low-quality low-price menu. Otherwise he will mimic the low-type by selecting the menu offered to the low-type.

Referring back to Figure 3.3, suppose the monopolist offers the menu to the low-type corresponding to the tangency point e_1' along its IR constraint Oa_1 and the menu to the high-type corresponding to the tangency point e_2' along its SS constraint passing through e_1'. But this separating menu, where the monopolist offers the same qualities to the two types of consumers as the competitive industry, does not maximize his total profit. If he offers a lower quality to the low-type consumer such as the one corresponding to e_1', he can extract greater surplus from the high-type consumer by pushing him at e_2' on the higher indifference curve $e_1''e_2''$. It can easily be checked that this raises the monopolist's profit from catering to the high-type more than he loses from catering such a lower quality at a lower price to the low-type. Thus, at a separating equilibrium, the monopolist will degrade the quality offered to the low-type consumers.

The extent to which he degrades the quality at the low-end of the market, however, depends on the distribution pattern. If the low type consumers are significantly large in number, the monopolist will not degrade the quality much. Otherwise quality distortion will be large. To derive the exact condition, note that by the IR constraint for the low-type consumers, p_1 must be such that,

$$u(\alpha_1, p_1) = p_1 \tag{3.12}$$

and by the SS constraint of the high-type, p_2 must be such that,

$$p_2 = u(\alpha_2, q_2) - u(\alpha_2, q_1) + u(\alpha_1, q_1) \tag{3.13}$$

so the profit of the monopolist from the separating menu or quality discrimination equals,

$$\pi = n_1[u(\alpha_1, q_1) - c(q_1)] + n_2[\mathrm{u}(\alpha_2, q_2) - u(\alpha_2, q_1) + u(\alpha_1, q_1) - c(q_2)] \tag{3.14}$$

It is straightforward to check that,

$$\frac{\partial \pi}{\partial q_1} = [(n_1 + n_2)u_q(\alpha_1, q_1) - n_2 u_q(\alpha_2, q_1) - n_1 c_q(q_1)] \tag{3.15}$$

which is negative if,

$$\frac{n_1}{n_2} \leq \frac{u_q(\alpha_2, q_1) - u_q(\alpha_1, q_1)}{u_q(\alpha_1, q_1)} \forall q \in [0, \bar{q}] \tag{3.16}$$

Given non-decreasing marginal utility of quality, this is satisfied if,

$$\frac{n_1}{n_2} \leq \frac{u_q(\alpha_2, \bar{q}) - u_q(\alpha_1, \bar{q}_1)}{u_q(\alpha_1, \bar{q}_1)} \tag{3.16a}$$

Thus if the distribution of the consumers across different types satisfies (3.16a), the monopolist caters only to the high type and extracts whole of their surplus by pushing them to their IR constraint. Note that this condition may be satisfied even when the consumers are uniformly distributed (i.e., $n_1 = n_2$).

What remains to be shown is that if the market is fully covered with a separating menu, then the quality offered to the low-type is degraded by the monopolist relative to the competitive quality. To see this, evaluate (3.15) at the competitive quality q_{1C} such that $u_q(\alpha_1, q_{1C}) = c_q(q_{1C})$:

$$\left.\frac{\partial \pi}{\partial q_1}\right|_{q_{1C}} = n_2[u_q(\alpha_1, q_{1C}) - u_q(\alpha_2, q_{1C})] \tag{3.17}$$

But by (3.10b), the right hand side is negative. Hence, by the second order condition for maximum, the profit-maximizing quality offered to the low type is strictly lower than the competitive quality.

A few comments are warranted at this point. First, if the restrictions on the cost structure do not satisfy a condition similar to (3.8) for the high-type, there does not exist any separating menu that maximizes the monopolist's profit. He then offers a pooling menu with the topmost quality to both the types. The typical example of such a solution is when both the preference and cost structure is linear [Acharyya (1998)]. This result is independent of the number of types or whether consumers are distributed discretely or continuously over the types (see appendix). Second, if anything, the extent of the market coverage by the monopolist is an equilibrium outcome rather than an ex ante restriction. Regardless of whether a separating menu or a pooling menu is to be offered in case the market is fully covered, i.e., regardless of condition (3.8), the monopolist will not cover the market fully *at equilibrium* if the distribution pattern satisfies (3.16a) in the two-type case. For $k > 2$ types, similar condition can be derived for which the top $(k - n)$ types are catered to.

Third, costs may influence the above set of results in another important way. As demonstrated by Kim and Kim (1996), when costs involve positive spillover effects in the sense that the production of high quality variety lowers the cost of lower quality variety, the high-type consumers may be offered a lower quality than the low-type at the socially optimum equilibrium. This is contrary to the standard result derived in Figure 3.3. Moreover, under such circumstances the monopolist may offer a pooling menu with a uniform quality that lies between the two socially optimum qualities. Thus, unlike the standard case, quality distortion occurs for both types. However, for the high-type the quality is enhanced whereas for the low-type the quality is degraded.

In fact, even without any spillover effect in costs, there may be quality distortion at the top if total and marginal utilities are negatively rather than positively correlated. This of course, violates the standard assumptions made in (3.10). Srinagesh and Bradburd (1989) demonstrate such a non-standard possibility in a situation where consumers, with varying levels of efficiency, produce commodities with inputs of purchased goods and time similar to Becker's (1965) production structure.

The standard analysis set out above and its variants use two assumptions. First is that the consumers differ in respect of their tastes but have identical incomes. Second, consumers do not face any purchasing power constraint in the sense that all of them can afford to pay even the highest quality when charged the maximum price that extracts all of their surplus. The first assumption, the basis of consumer heterogeneity, does not really matter as pointed out by Tirole (1989). In fact the above analyses hold even if we assume that the taste parameter α, which influence the marginal willingness-to-pay for quality, is an increasing function of the income parameter $\theta \in [\underline{\theta}, \overline{\theta}]$, so that the high income consumers have higher taste and hence higher marginal willingness-to-pay for quality than the low income consumers. Thus, income disparities per se do not matter. However, the second assumption is critical particularly when consumer heterogeneity is defined in terms of income disparity. Under such circumstances, it may not appear to be too reasonable to assume ex ante that even some low income consumers can afford to pay for the highest quality, though ex post, i.e., at equilibrium, the monopolist may offer a price that may enable them to purchase that quality. This is particularly important for the product categories that are often exemplified in these types of models, such as, cars, refrigerators and other consumer durables.

What is important to note is that under such a binding purchasing power constraint, even if the marginal willingness-to-pay does not vary with the income levels, and all consumers have identical taste and hence identical marginal willingness-to-pay, there is the possibility of quality discrimination and differentiation. Figure 3.4 illustrates this point[7]. Suppose θ_1 be the income of the low-income consumer and θ_2 be the income of the high-income consumer, and $\theta_1 < \theta_2$. All the consumers, however, have identical taste represented by the same taste parameter α. Thus, the marginal willingness-to-pay for both the low and high income is assumed to be same. This leads to the same individual-rationality constraint, given by the straight line Oa (representing linear preference structure), for both the types. Of course, this assumption is just to demonstrate that with binding purchasing power constraints in the sense defined below, it is possible to obtain quality discrimination at equilibrium even though all consumers have identical marginal willingness-to-pay.

Let the purchasing power constraint be binding for the low-type consumers for qualities $q \in [\tilde{q}_1, \overline{q}]$. Thus, the market participation constraint for the low-type consumers is given by the kinked curve Oe_1b_1. Till $\tilde{q}_1$ the individual-rationality constraint is binding and accordingly the low-type consumer's purchase or market participation decision is based on net utility derived or on the willingness-to-pay. But for quality levels beyond that, the purchasing power constraint is binding and accordingly the purchase decision now is based on the consumer's ability-to-pay. Clearly, for cost curve such as $c(q)$, the monopolist offers the quality $\tilde{q}_1 = \theta_1/\alpha$ to the low-income type and charges the price $p_1 = \theta_1$ that extracts all the surplus (and

[7] See Acharyya (2004) for an elaborate analysis.

the income) from them. Given that the low-income consumers cannot afford-to-pay a price greater than θ_1, the monopolist can now offer any price-quality menu along the e_1a segment of the individual-rationality constraint to the high-income consumers.

Of course, which particular menu it will offer to them depends on the level of θ_2. If it is less than θ_2'', such as θ_2', so that the purchasing power constraint is binding for the high-income consumers as well, the monopolist offers the quality $\tilde{q}_2 = \theta_2/\alpha$, and charges θ_2. Otherwise, it offers them the topmost quality. In any case, the monopolist adopts a separating menu (quality discrimination) and a sufficient condition for this is that the purchasing power constraint is binding for the low-income consumers in the sense defined above.

What is to be noted is that now for any positive cost of quality, regardless of how fast such cost increases with quality, separating menu exists and will be the profit-maximizing menu. In fact, regardless of the convexity of cost of quality, the monopolist will always offer the quality $\tilde{q}_1$ to the low-income type and a strictly higher quality to the high-income type.

3.3 Low-Quality Phenomena in LDCs: Application of the Benchmark Model

The benchmark models described above can be extended to explain quality differences across countries and low-quality phenomena in the developing

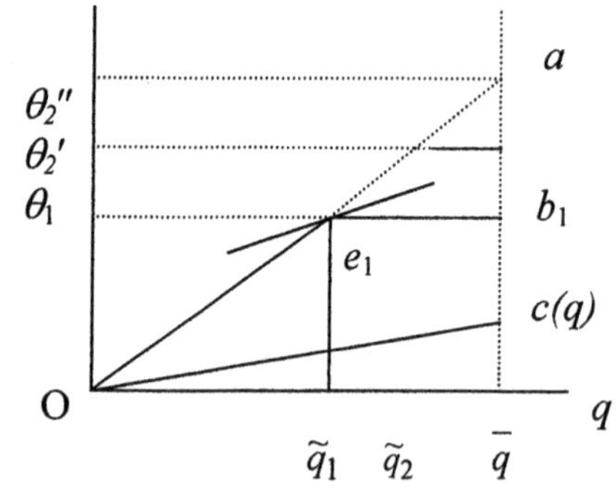

Figure 3.4: Purchasing Power Constraint and Quality Discrimination

countries. More precisely, both the technological asymmetry and demand asymmetry arguments for such phenomena can well be captured through the benchmark models.

3.3.1 Technology Asymmetry and Role of Research & Development

Technological disadvantage of the developing countries is a major explanation of the low quality of their products. Such technological constraint may arise in two ways. First, the marginal cost of quality is higher resulting in lower quality chosen by the domestic producers. Referring to Figure 3.4, suppose consumers in a developing country (home) and in a developed country (foreign) are alike with respect to both tastes and incomes. Thus the same set of indifference curves captures the preference structure of the consumers in both these countries. Clearly, a higher marginal cost of quality at home, as reflected in a steeper $c(q)$ curve, which will imply selection of a lower quality than that abroad. Moreover, if $c(q)$ lies wholly above $c^*(q)$ as in Figure 3.4, which implies absolute cost advantage of firms in the developed country, then in case the home or the developing-country market is liberalized, the domestic consumers will buy from the firms in the developed country as that will entail them higher net utility (along $a_1''a_1''$).

Second, the firms in the developing country may have the same cost curve as those in the developed countries, but the technology available to them may just allow them to produce goods with varieties strictly less than q_C^*. That is, here the technological asymmetry is such that the range of qualities that the firms at home can produce is only a lower subset of the qualities that the producers abroad can produce. In terms of Figure 3.5 this would mean that the cost curve faced by the firms at home is $cK\tilde{c}(q)$. Thus, pre-trade, the firms in the developing country offer $\tilde{q}$, which is lower than the quality $\tilde{q}$ * in the developed country.

In either case, the technological constraint explains the low-quality phenomena in the developing countries. Investment in R&D or innovation, cost-innovation in the former case and quality-innovation in the latter, under such circumstances relaxes the technological constraint. This is the basis of the popular argument that due to very low levels of R&D, product qualities are poor in the developing countries. There are indeed quite a handful of evidences regarding low levels of R&D expenditure or innovations in the developing countries.

Table 3.1 reports such expenditures as a percentage of Gross National Product (GNP) for a selected group of developed and developing countries during 1986-1996. France, Germany, Japan and the US have spent around 2.5 percent of their respective GNP on the average on R&D, whereas for Australia, Canada and the UK, such spending were around 2 percent on the average over the entire period.

But the developing countries, except Korea, lag far behind. Only India and Brazil spent a little less than one percent of their GNP on R&D. However, for India, the growth of R&D expenditure had fallen behind that of its GNP, resulting in a falling share of R&D expenditure. Performances of China, Indonesia and Sri Lanka are even worse. They have spent less than one-half percent of their GNP on R&D. Thus, there has been a wide variation in the R&D efforts across the developed and the developing countries.

However, the low levels of R&D expenditure as an explanation of low quality in the developing countries must also explain why R&D expenditures are low in the developing countries in the first place. There are several competing arguments for that. One explanation is the demand story: Structure of demand in a country, both in terms of size of the market and willingness-to-pay, determines the level of R&D investment.

In a very simple way this argument has been captured in Acharyya and Roy Chowdhury (2004). Consider the following decision making process of a monopolist in a market with identical consumers having marginal willingness-to-pay equal to α.

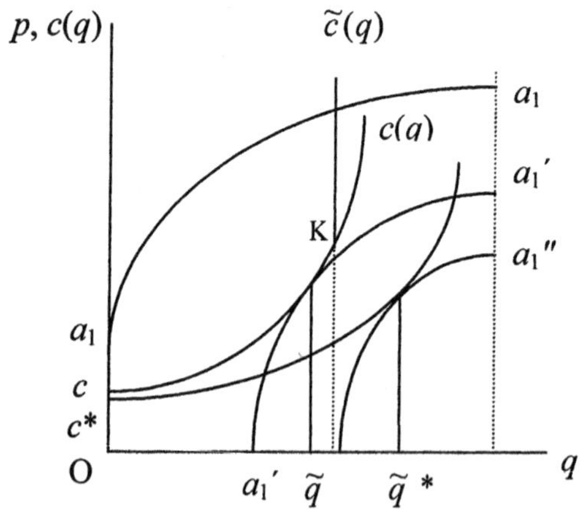

Figure 3.5: Cost Asymmetry and Quality Variation

He first develops a range of qualities $[0, \tilde{q}]$ through R&D and then selects a quality from amongst this set to maximize his profit. Suppose the R&D is certain and involves a one-time cost F which rises proportionately with the level of topmost quality innovated:

$$F = \delta q, \ \delta > 0 \tag{3.18}$$

Table 3.1: R&D Expenditure as a Percentage of GNP

	1986	1988	1994	1995	1996
Australia	1.4	1.3	1.72		1.8
Brazil	0.4		0.82	0.84	0.81
Canada	1.5		1.69	1.6	1.65
China			0.8	0.5	
France	2.3	2.3		2.37	2.33
Germany	2.27		2.31	2.3	2.3
India	0.95	0.96	0.71	0.8	0.66
Indonesia	0.3	0.2	0.07	0.1	
Japan	2.8	2.8	2.9		
Korea Rep.	1.8	1.9	2.6	2.71	2.82
Mexico			0.22	0.31	0.31
Sri Lanka	0.19		0.14		0.18
UK	2.3		2.12	2.04	1.95
USA	2.8	2.9	2.52	2.61	2.54
Turkey		0.5	0.36	0.38	

Sources: Science & Technology Pocket Data Book 2000, Ministry of Science and Technology, GOI; National Survey of Research & Development in Sri Lanka 1996.

The firms face no production cost whatsoever once qualities are developed. For any given range of qualities developed, it is straightforward to check that the monopolist will push them to their reservation utility by charging $p = u(\alpha, q)$ for any quality, and will offer the technologically feasible topmost quality $\tilde{q}$. This follows from the assumption of zero production cost as explained earlier. Formally, the monopolist selects a quality from $[0, \tilde{q}]$ to maximize its profit $nu(\alpha, q)$, where n is the number of home consumers. Since by the marginal utility is increasing in quality, $u_q(\alpha, q) > 0$, the profit is maximized at $q = \tilde{q}$. The first stage decision for the monopolist thus boils down to innovating the topmost quality level $\tilde{q}$ which maximizes his profit net of the R&D cost: $nu(\alpha, \tilde{q}) - \delta q$. The topmost innovated quality level $\bar{q}$ is the solution of the following first order condition:

$$u_q(\alpha, \bar{q}) = \frac{1}{n}\delta \tag{3.19}$$

Figure 3.6 illustrates the innovation decision of the home firm. It is immediate that since marginal utility (which is here the marginal revenue) is diminishing in quality level, so the monopolist will innovate a higher level of quality if it faces a larger set of consumers or a greater market for its product. A larger market means the marginal cost, δ, spreads over a larger set of consumers and this raises the incentives for innovating a higher level of quality. Similarly, higher will be the level of innovation, higher is the marginal willingness-to-pay for quality. To explain the cross-country differences in innovation and consequent technology (or quality) levels, consider similar decision of a firm in a foreign country which has similar structure as the home country except that consumers there have a higher total as well as marginal willingness-to-pay. Thus, foreign consumers are of high *type*. With number of foreign consumers being n^*, the foreign monopolist's innovated topmost quality for the foreign market $\bar{q}^*$ would be the solution of the following profit-maximizing condition:

$$u_q(\alpha^*, \bar{q}^*) = \frac{1}{n^*}\delta \tag{3.20}$$

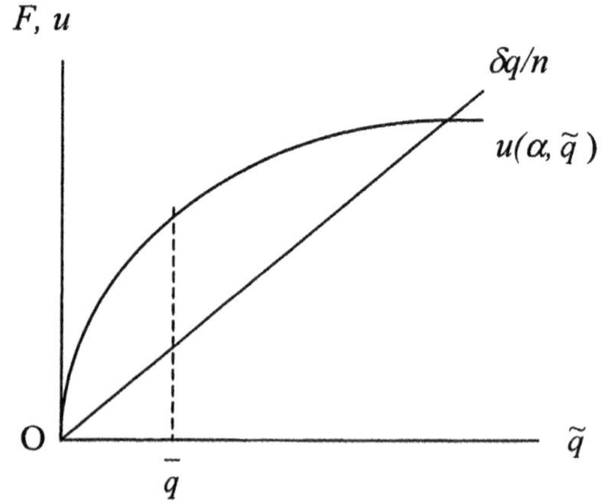

Figure 3.6: Market Size and Innovation Level

It is now straightforward to check that our home country will develop a lower level of quality if it has a smaller market size or, when it has a larger market size, if the relative market size is smaller than a critical level as defined below:

$$\frac{n}{n^*} < \frac{u_q(\alpha^*, \bar{q}^*)}{u_q(\alpha, \bar{q}^*)} \tag{3.21}$$

Note, by the property of the preference function defined earlier, the above condition is satisfied even when $n > n^*$. Since usually the developing countries have a relatively large number of consumers with low marginal willingness-to-pay, this offers a simple explanation of the observed technology gap between developing and developed countries.

Another oft quoted explanation of low R&D expenditure and innovation level in developing countries is that the protective trade policies eliminates foreign competition and thereby lowers the incentive for innovations whatsoever [Lall (1984), Acharyya (1995), and Marjit and Raychaudhuri (1997)]. The argument can be formalized along the following lines. Consider the simplest case of two varieties of the product, low quality (*L*) and high quality (*H*). A domestic monopolist, for example, has the technology to produce the low-quality variety but not the high-quality variety. In order to produce the high quality, it must invest a fixed amount F in an R&D project with success rate ρ. Suppose the domestic market for the low-quality good is protected through a non-prohibitive ad-valorem tariff, t. As long as the tariff-inclusive price of the import of low-quality variety, $(1+t)p^*$, is less than the monopoly price in the domestic market, the domestic monopolist can charge no more than the tariff-inclusive price and essentially acts as if he is a price-taker. Thus he serves the entire market at the price given in the world market when its marginal cost is constant. For example, for a tariff rate t_0, the domestic monopolist charges the price $(1+t_0)p^*$ and supplies $x(t_0)$. It can then be easily verified that the corresponding profit function has the following property:

$$\pi_L = \begin{cases} \pi_L(t) & \forall t < \bar{t} \\ \pi_{mL} & \forall t \geq \bar{t} \end{cases} \tag{3.18}$$

where $\pi_L(t) = [(1+t)p^* - c]D(1+t)p^*)$.

At the other extreme, when the tariff rate equals or exceeds the critical rate $\bar{t}$ such that $(1+\bar{t})p^* = p_m$, the domestic firm can exercise its monopoly power and since the monopoly profit is unique, charges the price p_m for all such tariff rates and earns π_{mL}. For tariff rates lower than $\bar{t}$, however, the domestic firm is a price-taker and earns $\pi_L(t)$ which increases with the tariff rate. Suppose, the world market for the low-quality variety is perfectly competitive and that the domestic monopolist has the same marginal cost as the foreign firms. Thus, π_L is zero when imports are free.

On the other hand, to keep things simple, suppose that only one foreign firm operates in the home-country market for the high-quality variety. This may be a reflection of the imperfect nature of the world market or the outcome of the restricted-entry policy of the home government. However, the number of foreign firms operating in the high-end of the domestic market really does not affect qualitatively what I show below, as long as there are super-normal profits that can be reaped by a late entrant. If the domestic firm does not innovate or is unsuccessful in developing the high-quality variety through innovation, the foreign firm earns the monopoly profit π^*_{mH}. But when the domestic firm successfully innovates, it can compete with the foreign firm. Assuming Cournot competition among them in such a case, the gross profit that the domestic firm can derive is the Cournot-duopoly profit π_{dH}.

Given such profit alternatives π_L and π_{dH}, and the assumption that if the firm successfully innovates then it switches to production of the high-quality good, the expected profit of the domestic firm from innovation equals:

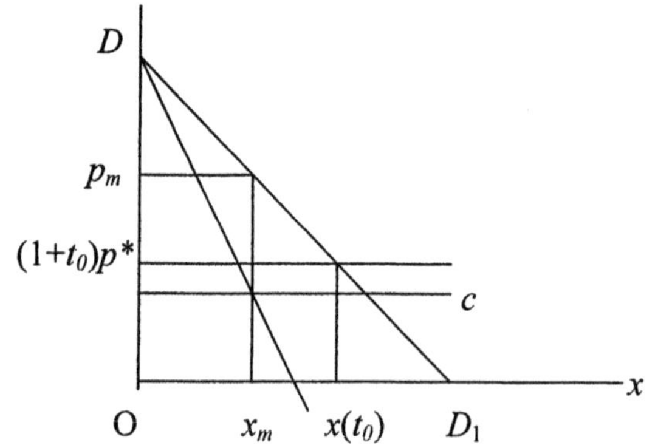

Figure 3.7: Domestic Monopolist's Output Decision

$$E\pi = \rho\pi_{dH} + (1-\rho)\pi_L - F \tag{3.19}$$

Given (3.18), the expected profit from innovation varies inversely with the tariff rate and with the level of R&D investment. Of course, the values of the parameter are such that the expected profit is positive. Otherwise, innovation is not viable and hence will not be undertaken. But, this alone is not a sufficient condition for innovation decision. The firm innovates only if the expected profit is as large as what it gets by not innovating, π_L:

$$R\pi = \rho[\pi_{dH} - \pi_L] - F \geq 0 \tag{3.20}$$

where, $R\pi$ is the relative profit from innovation.

Figure 3.8 illustrates the innovation decision, where $\tilde{F}$ and $\hat{F}$ are obtained by setting $E\pi$ and $R\pi$ to zero respectively. These are the critical values of the fixed R&D cost that define the regions where innovation is viable and relatively profitable. The particular shapes of these curves follow from the property of the π_L function defined in (3.18). Of course, we assume that $\pi_{mL} > \pi_{dH}$, such that for some tariff rate lower than $\tilde{t}$, $\hat{F} = \pi_{dH} - \pi_L(t) = 0$. The R&D region is, therefore, the area between the curve labeled $\hat{F}$ and the two axes. Thus for any combination of fixed cost $F \in [0, \rho\pi_{dH}]$ and the tariff rate $t \in [0, \tilde{t}]$, the domestic firm innovates. Otherwise innovation is relatively unprofitable.

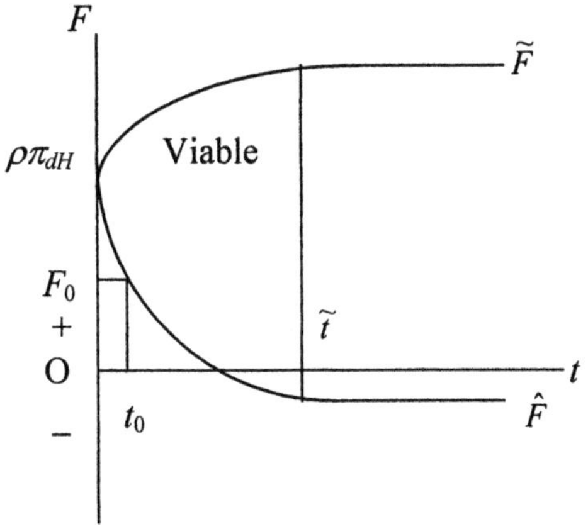

Figure 3.8: Tariff and Innovation Decision

For example, for $F = F_0$, if the tariff on low-quality import is higher than t_0, the firm will not innovate even though innovation is viable. This is the basis of the argument that a protective domestic market is not conducive for innovation. Of course, if the success rate is very high, then even a high tariff can sustain innovation. But the central message is that, given the rate of success, protection beyond a critical level erodes all the incentives for innovation. This result can easily be generalized to the case of more than one domestic and one foreign firm. As long as the firms compete in Cournot fashion, the essence of the argument remains unchanged.

In many countries, not only in the advanced industrialized countries but also in countries like India, low-quality imports are often subject to tariff and non-tariff barriers. Short run benefits and welfare implications of such policies are quite understandable. But what the above argument indicates, such policies in the long run may work against the competitiveness of domestic firms by discouraging them to switch to production of higher quality varieties of these products through innovation process. There is thus a conflict between short run gains and long run losses from such a protective policy.

But not always trade liberalization encourages innovation. That trade protection, instead of liberalization, might be conducive for innovation in some particular situations has been demonstrated by quite a few researchers [Clemenz (1991), Reitzes (1991), Rodrik (1992), Acharyya and Bandyopadhyay (2004)]. One such case is when consumers are heterogeneous and value quality enhancement of a product differently from each other. To explain, refer back to the earlier developed quality-choice framework with two types of consumers. As explained earlier, given certain restrictions on the distribution of consumers across types, the monopolist will offer a separating menu. But suppose the present state of technology available to the monopolist does not allow him to offer such a separating menu. In particular, suppose the topmost quality permissible by the present state of technology that he possesses is just the optimal quality he would offer to the low type. Without innovation, he must therefore offer this quality to both types. He can discriminate among different types by offering a separating menu and reap a higher profit only through successful innovation of higher qualities. However, when imports are not prohibited, the monopoly power of the domestic firm is restricted and this reduces the gain from quality discrimination and therefore from innovation. A reduction of tariff on low-quality imports forces the domestic firm to lower price not only of its low-quality variety but also of the high-quality variety, if *innovated* at all, to make the menus incentive compatible. Thus the monopolist understands that after successful innovation he can extract a smaller surplus from the high-type consumers when tariff on low-quality imports is lowered and is thus discouraged to innovate. A higher tariff on low quality imports, on the other hand, enables the domestic firm to raise price of such variety, and consequently to raise the price of the high-quality variety as well along the higher self-selection constraint of the high-type consumers. It is because of this scope of extracting more surplus from the high-type through innovation that a higher tariff on low-quality imports increases the incentive for quality innovation.

The essence of the above discussions is that the favourable (or adverse) impact of trade liberalization on innovation decision to remove the technological constraint on quality enhancement depends much on the characteristics of the market.

3.3.2 Income Disparity

Income disparity across the developing and the industrialized countries can also be a plausible explanation for quality differences. Qualities may be different because of differences in both the willingness-to-pay and constraining dimensions of cross-country per-capita income differences. For example, qualities may be different across countries when differences in their incomes per capita result in the differences in the marginal willingness-to-pay. To illustrate, suppose the taste parameter α is an increasing function of the income. Also assume that in each of the two countries under consideration, all consumers are alike, but domestic consumers have low incomes per capita than the foreign consumers: $\theta_1 < \theta_2$. Referring back to Figure 3.3, if competitive producers in both the countries share the same technology represented by the cost curve $c(q)$, the lower quality q_{1C} will be offered in the domestic country and the higher quality q_{2C} will be provided in the foreign country.

On the other hand, even if marginal willingness-to-pay does not depend on incomes, as is the case when preference pattern of consumers (as captured by the taste parameter α) is income independent, constraining effect of income by itself mean different qualities being offered in the two countries. Referring back to Figure 3.4, it is immediate that a lower quality $\tilde{q}_1$ will be offered in the country with lower per capita income θ_1 and a higher quality $\tilde{q}_2$ in the country with higher per capita income θ_2'.

3.4 Unobservable Quality, Information and Reputation: Alternative Explanations

The quality problem in case of goods with unobservable qualities has an altogether different dimension than discussed above. In such cases, moral hazard and adverse selection by producers explain much of the low-quality phenomena in the developing countries. Absence of perfect warranty system, high cost of maintaining reputation through high quality and information externality prohibit the producers in the developing countries to overcome these moral hazard and adverse selection problems. In this section we briefly review these explanations.

3.4.1 Asymmetric Information and Product Quality

There are many goods for which consumers cannot judge the quality before purchasing and experiencing these goods. Almost all the durable goods fall into this category of experience goods[8]. Among the non-durables, typical examples are that of canned food, quality of food in a restaurant, quality of service in a hotel and the like.

In all these cases, how the consumers learn about qualities and the incentives for firms to supply the quality that they announce are the main problems rather than the selection of a particular quality. Essentially in markets for these goods we have the moral hazard and adverse selection (or lemons) problems on part of the producers.

In absence of repeat purchase by consumers, as for example in case of durables, and with limited or no warranty system, there is no way the consumers can learn about the quality of the product before purchase. Under such circumstances, the price the consumers like to pay for the good is independent of the true quality of the good. This leads to the moral hazard problem on part of the producers: They will supply the lowest quality as long as the cost of quality is increasing. Since consumers purchase only once, there is no incentive for the producers to build up reputation by providing high quality. On the other hand, in absence of any warranty system, they do not have to be bothered about compensation either in case of poor performance of the low-quality good that they offer.

---

[8] Darby and Karni (1973) distinguish further between experience and credence goods. In case of credence goods, not all aspects of quality can be judged even after consumption, such as the amount of chemical flavour in a sweet.

What remains, therefore, is the savings upon costs by providing the lowest quality. Of course, the market may collapse when the maximum price that the monopolist can charge for such a quality, αq, does not cover the cost, cq.

The moral hazard problem can be avoided if we have a full warranty system. When the performance of a good can entirely be attributed to the intrinsic quality of the good, a less-than-full warranty signals low quality. But the warranty systems are not always perfect for a variety of reasons and in fact in many cases full warranty system can lead to moral hazard problem on part of the consumers. So warranty system may not be a plausible solution of the above problem. We shall return to this later.

Sequential purchase of the good with a positive probability that the new buyers meet the old buyers before making their choices for a particular product, or existence of some buyers having private information regarding the true quality of the good, however, can overcome the moral hazard problem to a large extent. Since the informed buyers pay according to the quality of the good that they could assess based on their private information, there is now a loss of revenue from these consumers not buying the product if the low quality is offered by the producer. The producer thus weighs this loss against the savings upon cost while deciding upon providing a low quality. As Tirole (1989) nicely puts it with the help of a simple example, there are two implications. First, larger is the proportion of the informed buyers, more likely is that the producer offers the higher quality. Second, for the uninformed buyers, a high price offers a high quality because they correctly anticipate that the producer can induce the informed buyers to buy his product by charging a high price only when he offers a high quality.

Adverse selection, or what Akerlof (1970) termed lemons problem, arises when the producer decides about whether to put the good into the market for sale or to hold back for self-consumption. Once again, since the price that the consumers will be willing to pay is independent of the quality of the good, because they cannot observe the quality a priori, the producer will be putting the good into the market only when it is of low quality. Otherwise, he is better off by consuming the good by himself. This is typically the case in the market for used cars in the US where the bad cars (called lemons) are put to sale. In a sense, due to such adverse selection, bad quality drives out good quality from the market.

3.4.2 Reputation, Contestability and Information Externality

Reputation is often seen as a possible way of overcoming the moral hazard problem in a market with repeated purchases [Allen (1984), Klein and Leffler (1981), Shapiro (1983)]. Markets for non-durables are the cases where consumers make repeated purchases. In such cases the consumers use the quality of the goods produced by a firm in the past as an indicator of the present or future quality. Thus, firms' decisions to supply a quality become essentially a dynamic one. Firms that produce low-quality goods but sell at the high-quality prices, acquire a bad reputation and are excluded from the market in the future.

However, the loss or gain from reputation accrues only in the long run. In the short run, firms always have incentives to cut back quality which lowers cost and maximizes their profits. Thus, as Klein and Leffler (1981) argue, unless the future stream of positive premia from a strategy of maintaining a good reputation through high quality is quite high, there will be little incentive for firms to build reputation and overcome the moral hazard problem.

Herein emerges an alternative explanation of the low-quality phenomena in the developing countries. Most of the markets in the developing countries are characterized by many small producers with no sunk cost and consequently free and easy entry and exit. The markets thus resemble the features of contestable markets: The incumbents are vulnerable to hit-and-run entry should they ever try to exert their potential market power by raising prices above marginal costs. In such cases, there will be little scope and incentive for the incumbents to build reputation. The potential hit-and-run entrants, on the other hand, being transient in nature, entering the market whenever there is any profit opportunity and leaving once some profits are reaped, care little about how consumers regard quality.

Rashid (1988) provides quite a few examples of such contestability leading to low-quality phenomena beginning from the cloth industry in the UK in the pre Industrial Revolution period and in China in the nineteenth century, to supply of adulterated milk in Bangladesh and supply of rice mixed with pebbles in India in the present era. In all these markets, easy entry erodes any rent that sellers expect from their continued operation and thus reduces their incentives to maintain a good reputation through high quality. Esfahani (1991) provides a slightly different explanation for the quality puzzle in the developing countries. He argues that cost uncertainty and fluctuations and high interest rates raise the premium necessary to maintain high quality beyond a level that consumers can afford to pay.

In all these arguments, premium on reputation hold the center-stage, which are not reconcilable in highly competitive and contestable markets in the developing countries. Regulation and market concentration may, therefore, help firms build reputation. Similar conclusion has been arrived at by Chiang and Masson (1988) in the context of informational externality that the goods with unobservable qualities lead to. Based on Armington (1969) and Akerlof's (1970) ideas, the building bloc of their argument is that though the consumers cannot quite judge the quality of a particular product a priori, they have a perception of the average quality of the industry. Accordingly the price that they are willing to pay for the product is based on such perception of average industry quality. For example, only a few people will disagree that Swiss watches are good or that electronic goods produced in Japan are of high quality. Similarly, people have quite good perceptions regarding the average quality of cars produced in Japan and the US. Thus they would be willing to pay a high price for such goods even if they cannot assess the true quality of the products. But with a few exceptions like rice, textiles, and software, buyers in the advanced industrialized countries perceive that the average industry quality in the developing countries is poor and will therefore be willing to pay a lower price than those goods produced in the developed countries. Such perceptions discourage potential producers in the developing countries to offer a quality higher than the perceived average industry quality unless quality enhancement at the individual firm level raises the average industry quality level as well. This leads to the adverse selection problem where all producers offer low quality and consumers' perceptions are realized.

What is even worse, even if individual quality enhancement raises the average industry quality, due to the inherent informational externality, firms offer qualities lower than the socially optimum quality. The reason is simple. An individual producer equates its private marginal benefit with its private marginal cost of quality enhancement. The private marginal benefit is the additional price that the consumers are willing to pay due to consequent increase in the average industry quality. But this benefits other firms in the industry as well. Thus, there is a positive externality of quality enhancement by a particular firm. This makes the social marginal benefit higher than the private marginal benefit. Hence, the quality offered by an individual producer is less than the socially optimum quality.

Since the average industry quality depends on the number of firms in the industry, the obvious policy intervention is that of restricting the number of exporting firms. Generalizing the analysis, Donnenfeld and Mayer (1987) demonstrate that quantitative restrictions like the voluntary export restraints (VER) can also achieve the socially optimum quality. The weak link in these arguments, however, is the implicit assumption that the consumers can correctly assess the *actual* average industry quality. This assumption has quite a different implication than the assumption that the consumers can perceive that market concentration or VER raises the average industry quality and accordingly revise their willingness-to-pay upwards.

Once the consumers' perception about industry quality is equated with the *actual* average industry quality (which means that they can correctly assess the exact average industry quality), it is obvious that allowing only a single firm to operate in the industry will eliminate all the informational externality because now the private and marginal benefits will be the same. But, at the same time this contradicts the basic premise that quality of a product is unobservable because in case of a single firm the assumption that that consumers have perfect knowledge about the industry quality means that they know the quality of the good that this single firm produces as well. To avoid this logical inconsistency, if it is assumed that the consumers perceptions about the average industry quality is different from what the actual average industry quality is, then the problem of moral hazard remains in case of a single firm. Even though the consumers can correctly assess that market concentration raises the average industry quality level than before (but they may not know exactly how much it improves), the higher price that they will be willing to pay will still be lower than what they would have paid if they had full information regarding the actual quality. Consequently, the single producers will still have the moral hazard and adverse selection problems in regard to what quality to offer.

However, even though the moral hazard and adverse selection problems cannot altogether be overcome, market concentration or VER can certainly eliminate the information externality problem. But, restricting entry to the market and allowing concentration of firms, either to ensure the minimum premium required for maintaining a good reputation or to eliminate the informational externality, may not be socially desirable.

3.4.3 Quality Standards, Product Labeling and Information

There are two policies that can eliminate the information problem and consequently help overcome the moral hazard and adverse selection problems. First is the enforcement of full warranty system, and second is to impose the minimum quality standards and certify firms who comply by that.

Enforcement of a full warranty system, however, may not always work and sometimes may not even be desirable. Full warranty system eliminates the moral hazard problem on part of the producers when poor performance of a product can entirely be attributed to the intrinsic quality of the product. In fact, in such a case, the producer himself will offer full warranty and provide high quality. If he offers a less-than-full warranty, consumers correctly anticipate that the full warranty is not offered precisely because the good is of poor quality and hence is going to break down eventually. Therefore, less-than-full warranty signals low quality and no consumer buys the good from that producer.

But such a policy of full warranty has two problems. First, enforcement of a warranty system may not be fully feasible. Due to the subjective element in the quality aspect, even if poor performance of the good is observed by a consumer, it may not be fully assessed or measured by a court in order to comply the producer with its announced warranty. Thus, even announcing a full warranty a producer can get away with by providing a low quality. Second, if the eventual performance of a durable good depends as much on the way it is used by the consumer as on its intrinsic quality, then enforcement of a full warranty system is certainly not the first-best policy. This is because, full warranty system in such cases will lead to moral hazard problem on part of the consumers: They will care less about the maintenance of the good knowing that they will be fully compensated when the good breaks down even if that is due to their own mishandling rather than poor intrinsic quality of the good[9].

---

[9] In fact, it is due to such moral hazard problem on part of the consumers that we see producers offering limited warranty when they are free to choose the level and extent of warranty. There is also the adverse selection part of the problem: Limited warranty is chosen precisely to eliminate the high-risk consumers from the market. Because of all these, we observe, for example, no warranty on break down of computer systems due to virus or software related problems.

Minimum quality standards and product labeling, on the other hand, are more effective and easily implementable policy measures. By labeling the product that it attains a minimum quality standard, such as those set by ISO-9000 and ISO-14000, the producers can provide signal to the consumers about the true quality of their products. This encourages a potentially high-quality producer in the developing country to offer a quality higher than the average industry quality as it expects to get a higher price from the consumers because now they get the necessary information from the product label. It is precisely because of such positive information effect of product labeling that a growing number of firms are now observed to obtain the ISO certificates or eco-labels from the certifying bodies even though such certificates are costly both in terms of organizational restructuring and product standardization as well as in terms of application and process fees[10]. However, application and process fees are often not affordable for small producers in the developing countries. This is prohibiting them to obtain the quality certificates and get rid of the information problem. Given that the social marginal benefit of obtaining such certificates is much higher than the private marginal benefits, precisely because greater is the proportion of firms having quality-certificates better is the perception of the consumers regarding the average industry quality and consequently greater is their marginal-willingness-to-pay for any product in that industry, there is a need for governments in the developing countries to step forward by providing subsidies to cover at least a part of the cost of obtaining such certificates.

3.5 Conclusion

What emerges from the analyses in this chapter is that the market structure (distribution of consumers across different types, in particular), technology and information are the three major determinants of the quality of a product offered by firms. For search goods, technological constraint and low-income per capita explain the low-quality phenomena in the developing countries. Highly competitive and contestable markets and poor perceptions regarding the average industry quality, with the associated problems of information externality, in the developing countries, on the other hand, constitute the plausible explanations in the context of experience goods. Whereas the contestable markets erode the

[10] A survey on exporting firms in Bangladesh conducted by Raychaudhuri et. al. (2003) reveals such positive effects as 36 percent of these firms experienced an increase in their domestic as well as export sales.

incentives for maintaining good reputation to overcome the moral hazard problem for the producers, poor perceptions regarding average industry quality result in lower marginal willingness-to-pay for goods produced in the developing countries.

Three sets of trade and industrial policies appear to raise the product quality. A lowering of tariff on the low-quality imports may induce the firms in the developing countries to innovate which relax the technological constraint. Of course, the market for the high-quality variety must offer rent to the successful innovators. Otherwise, trade liberalization at the lower end of the market alone cannot induce innovation. Market concentration and/or export restrictions, on the other hand, affects quality choices in the developing countries in two ways. First, it ensures the premium for maintaining reputation by providing high quality. Second, it raises the foreign consumers' perceptions about the average industry quality and consequently their marginal willingness-to-pay. But from distribution aspect, allowing market concentration may not be desirable policy action. Minimum quality standards and product labeling, in contrast, are more effective measures to get rid of the information problem and to induce the producers to maintain a high quality of their products.

However, in a macroeconomic or general equilibrium context, in contrast to the partial equilibrium perspective of this chapter, liberal trade policies and/or product standards may have far reaching implications for income distribution and employment. Moreover, such policy effects may well be in conflict with the objective of quality enhancement and export growth. In the following chapters I focus on these issues.

Appendix

I. Cost Structure and the Pooling Menu: Discrete Case

To illustrate how the cost structure is important for a monopolist to offer a separating menu, let us assume the following specific forms of the utility and cost functions:

$$u(\alpha_j, q) = \alpha_j q,\ j = 1,2 \tag{A.3.1}$$

$$c(q) = \frac{1}{2}cq^2 \tag{A.3.2}$$

Given this linear utility function and convex cost of quality, it is straightforward to check that if the monopolist offers a separating menu $q_1^S < q_2^S$ then,

$$q_1^S = \frac{(n_1 + n_2)\alpha_1 - n_2\alpha_2}{n_1 c} \tag{A.3.3}$$

$$q_2^S = \frac{\alpha_2}{c} \tag{A.3.4}$$

Of course, the monopolist covers the market, i.e., serves both the types, if the distribution pattern is such that,

$$\frac{n_1}{n_2} \geq \frac{\alpha_2 - \alpha_1}{\alpha_1} \tag{A.3.5}$$

This is just the condition (3.16a) in the text under the linear preference function (A.3.1).

What appears from (A.3.3) and (A.3.4) is that both the quality levels vary inversely with the rate at which the cost increases with the quality, c. If cost does not increase sufficiently fast, $q_i^S = \bar{q} \;\forall\; j = 1,2$. Thus the monopolist offers the topmost quality to both types and hence a uniform price as well. That is, for (A.3.5) and a slowly increasing cost of quality, a *pooling menu* with topmost quality is offered at the equilibrium, even though the two types of consumers have different marginal willingness-to-pay.

What is the critical rate of increase in cost of quality for which such equilibrium occurs? To find, note that,

$$\frac{\partial \pi}{\partial q_1} = (n_1 + n_2)\alpha_1 - n_2\alpha_2 - n_1 c q_1$$

$$\frac{\partial \pi}{\partial q_2} = n_2(\alpha_2 - c q_2)$$

A little manipulation of these conditions show that $\frac{\partial \pi}{\partial q_1} > 0 \;\forall\; q_1$ if,

$$\alpha_1 \geq \frac{n_1}{n_1+n_2} c\bar{q} + \frac{n_2}{n_1+n_2}\alpha_2 \tag{A.3.6}$$

and $\frac{\partial \pi}{\partial q_2} > 0 \ \forall \ q_2$ if,

$$\alpha_2 \geq c\bar{q} \tag{A.3.7}$$

The following diagram illustrates the different equilibria for (A.3.7).

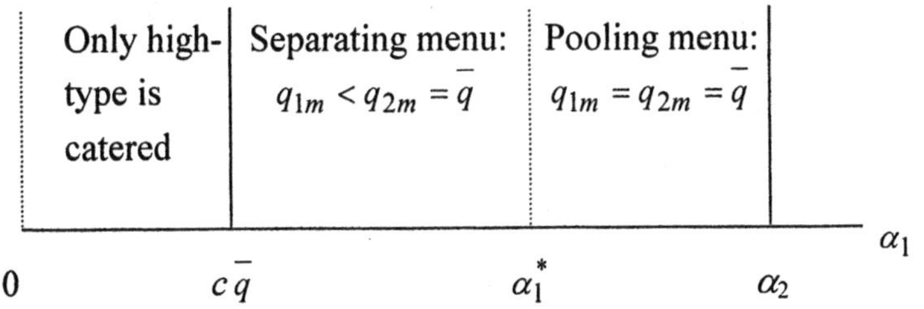

Figure 3.9: Equilibrium Menus for Different Parametric Configurations

Let the right hand side value in (A.3.6) be denoted by α_1^*. For $\forall \ \alpha_1 \in [\alpha_1^*, \alpha_2]$, the monopolist offers the pooling menu with topmost quality. Only for $\forall \ \alpha_1 \in [c\bar{q}, \alpha_1^*]$, the monopolist offers a separating menu. But since $\alpha_2 > c\bar{q}$, it offers the topmost quality to the high-type. As the rate of increase in the cost of quality increases, i.e., as the value of c increases, α_1^* increases too, so that the range of values of α_1 for which we have a pooling equilibrium shrinks as well.

Now suppose $\alpha_2 < c\bar{q}$. Thus $q_{2m} < \bar{q}$. That is, given the curvature property of the cost function and for (A.3.2), $c\underline{q} = 0 < \alpha_2$, there exists a $q_{2m} \ni \alpha_2 = cq_{2m}$. In such a case, however, $\alpha_1 < c\bar{q}$ as well. Therefore, a sufficient condition for a separating menu with interior qualities is that,

$$c\bar{q} > \alpha_2 \tag{A.3.8}$$

For preference and cost functions defined in (3.1) and (3.5) in the text, the sufficient conditions for such an equilibrium is that the marginal cost of the topmost quality must exceed the marginal utility of the topmost quality for the high type whereas the marginal cost for the lowest quality must be strictly less than the marginal utility of the lowest quality for the low-type:

$$c_q(\bar{q}) > u_q(\alpha_2, \bar{q}) \qquad \text{(A.3.9)}$$

$$c_q(0) < u_q(\alpha_1, 0) \qquad \text{(A.3.10)}$$

The condition (A.3.10) ensures that at equilibrium, the low-type is offered a quality which is strictly greater that the lowest quality. Otherwise, the low-type is either offered the lowest quality or not served at all. This condition, together with (3.16a), or (A.3.7), opens up an interesting possibility. If exactly the opposite inequality in (A.3.9) holds and $c_q(0) = u_q(\alpha_1, 0)$, a separating menu is offered where the low-type consumers get the lowest quality and the high-type consumers get the topmost quality. The quality discrimination is maximum and is similar to the bang-bang solution of Laffont and Tirole (1993) in a monopoly market and the maximum differentiation solution of Shaked and Sutton (1982) in an oligopolistic market.

II. Continuum of Consumer Types

Convexity of cost function is equally important when consumers are continuously distributed over different types and are not income constrained in the sense defined above. Once again, of course, it matters less when consumers, at least some of them, are income constrained. To illustrate, consider first the standard Mussa-Rosen specification with incomes not binding. Suppose consumers are distributed uniformly with density h over the interval $[0, \bar{\alpha}]$ specifying the range of their taste parameter. If the monopolist offers a uniform menu (p, q) to all consumers then his problem is to choose such a menu which maximizes his profit which equals,

$$\pi[p - c(q)]x \qquad \text{(A.3.11)}$$

where,

$$x = \int_{\alpha^*}^{\bar{\alpha}} f(\alpha)d\alpha = h[\bar{\alpha} - \alpha^*]$$

The marginal consumers defined by $\alpha^* = p/q$, are indifferent between buying and not buying the good. All consumers of higher type derive strictly positive net utility and therefore participate in the market. The marginal consumers also participate given the tie-breaking rule. Thus for any (pooling) menu, total demand equals $h[\overline{\alpha} - \alpha^*] = h[\overline{\alpha} - p/q]$. For any given choice of price, quality variation affects profit of the monopolist as,

$$\frac{\partial \pi}{\partial q} = h\left[-c'(q)\left(\overline{\alpha} - \frac{p}{q} \right) + \{p - c(q)\} \frac{p}{q^2} \right] \qquad \text{(A.3.12)}$$

It is immediate that $\partial\pi/\partial q > 0$ if $c'(q) = 0$, meaning that the topmost available quality $\overline{q}$ will maximize the monopolist's profit for any given positive price. The profit-maximizing price then can be obtained by setting $\partial\pi/\partial p = 0$ for $q = \overline{q}$:

$$p = \frac{1}{2}\left[\overline{\alpha q} + c(\overline{q})\right]$$

In fact, even for $c'(q) > 0$ monopolist's profit may be strictly increasing in quality over the feasible range. The cost function is similarly important when the monopolist offers separating menus to discriminate among different types of consumers.

III. Income Constrained Consumers

Consider the following simple extension of income-constrained consumers discussed in the text. Suppose consumers are distributed over the income range $[\underline{\theta}, \overline{\theta}]$ with density function $f(\theta)$ defined to be strictly positive for all income levels in this range. But suppose all consumers have identical taste. Assuming that the marginal willingness-to-pay is independent of income levels and is determined solely by the taste or preference of consumers, this means all consumers, regardless of their income disparity, have identical marginal willingness-to-pay for quality. This assumption is, of course, made to focus on the constraining effect of income and the implication of income disparity per se. A more general case would have been the one where incomes have both the constraining and utility effects so that income disparity would mean both different purchasing power constraints and marginal willingness-to-pay schedules (or the individual rationality constraints).

Consider first the choice of quality level under a pooling menu. Denoting the common taste parameter or marginal willingness-to-pay by α, it follows from the argument illustrated in Figure 3.4 that for any chosen price such as $p_1 = \theta_1$, consumers with income equal to or greater than θ_1 will buy the good only when the quality that is being offered by the monopolist is at least $\tilde{q}_1$, where $\alpha\tilde{q}_1 = \theta_1$. That is, for any quality less than $\tilde{q}_1$, demand for the good is zero.

Thus, the demand function for the monopolist for any price-quality menu can be written as,

$$D = \begin{cases} 0 & \text{if} \quad q < p/\alpha \\ [F(\bar{\theta}) - F(\theta)] & \text{if} \quad q \geq p/\alpha \end{cases} \tag{A.3.13}$$

where, $F(\theta)$ is the cumulative distribution function.

But, as long as marginal cost of producing higher quality is strictly positive, any quality higher than $\tilde{q}_1$ lowers the monopolist's profit given the price p_1 $(= \theta_1)$. Thus a profit-maximizing monopolist offers exactly $\tilde{q}_1$. This reduces the monopolist's problem to,

$$\text{Max}_p \quad \pi = [p - c(p/\alpha)][F(\bar{\theta}) - F(p)] \tag{A.3.14}$$

The first-order condition for profit maximization yields,

$$(\alpha - c')[F(\bar{\theta}) - F(p^*)] = \alpha F'(p^*)[p^* - c(p^*/\alpha)] \tag{A.3.15}$$

where, p^* is the optimum choice. Since α must be greater than $c'(0)$ and $c'' \geq 0$ for all quality levels, and $f(\theta) = F'(\theta) > 0$ in its support, so,

$$F(\bar{\theta}) > F(p^*) \Rightarrow p^* < \bar{\theta} \tag{A.3.16}$$

Finally, since all consumers are income constrained means $\bar{\theta} < \alpha\bar{q}$, (A.3.16) implies that $q^* < \bar{q}$.

Therefore, regardless of how fast the marginal cost of producing higher qualities increase, a monopolist offers to the income constrained consumers a quality q^* which is strictly lower than the topmost quality under a pooling menu.

Following the same logic as in the text above, it is straightforward then to check that, income disparity among these income constrained consumers per se opens up the possibility of quality discrimination even though all consumers have the same marginal willingness-to-pay and the marginal cost does not increase with quality as fast as defined in (3.8) in the text.

4 Income Distribution, Trade Policy and Export Quality

4.1 Introduction

One central message of the earlier chapter was that the marginal cost of quality is usually high in the developing countries causing them to select a lower quality of exports. Low marginal productivity of factors used in the production of export good due to inferior technology is what considered to be contributing towards such high marginal cost, for a given set of factor prices. But even with identical technology as accessed by the producers in the developed countries, relative scarcity of some of the factors of production may cause higher marginal cost of quality and consequently lower export quality in the developing countries. In fact, it is often argued that since higher quality varieties are relatively intensive in use of physical or human capital, relative scarcity of these factors make the production of relatively poorer qualities cheaper and hence more profitable.

Such an issue can only be addressed in a general equilibrium framework, unlike that presented in Chapter 3, where factor prices and the cost of quality are endogenously determined. This is essentially the factor-proportions explanation of poor export quality in the developing countries similar to the Heckscher-Ohlin explanation of the pattern of trade between the developed and the developing countries. At the same time such an approach links income distribution and choice of export quality from the supply side in contrast to the demand-side analysis of Chapter 3. In fact, there has been a two-way causation between export quality and income distribution in an open economy. Just as the income distribution, or relative factor prices affect the choice of export quality, any change in export quality also affects income distribution. Moreover, following the celebrated Stolper-Samuelson theorem, since trade policies redistribute income within a country, there can be an additional channel through which such policies can be used to achieve internationally competitive export qualities. Drawing heavily from Acharyya and Jones (2001), this chapter addresses these issues.

In section 4.2 we develop the basic general equilibrium model with production of both traded and non-traded goods. The non-traded good, such as construction or hair cut, by definition, must be locally produced to meet the domestic demand. To the extent to which production of these goods require scarce factors of production used in the export sector, variations in their demand and production produce changes in factor prices and therefore the choice of export quality. Falvey and Kierzkowski (1987) and Flam and Helpman (1987) developed a similar general equilibrium approach where the demand effect instead of the supply side effect of the change in income distribution holds the center stage. Copeland and Kotwal (1996) and Murphy and Shleifer (1997), on the other hand, have examined the basis and gains from trade in quality differentiated good among countries with technology and/or income differences. But the effect of domestic income distribution on quality choices and pattern of trade is missing in their analyses. Of course, technology rather than factor proportions (and income distribution) had been their primary focus.

Section 4.3 and 4.4 focus on the two-way causation between income distribution and export quality. In section 4.5 we provide a justification for capital market liberalization in the developing countries. In face of domestic scarcity of capital required to produce higher quality goods, capital market liberalization keep the capital cost down and thus enables the firms in the developing countries to serve the emerging export markets where buyers prefer relatively higher quality goods.

4.2 Quality Selection and Wage Determination in a Small Open Economy

Consider a small open economy producing two traded goods, T and Z, and a non-traded good, N. There are three (domestic) factors of production: skilled workers (S), unskilled labour (L) and physical capital (K). Endowments of these factors are given exogenously[11]. Whereas the skilled workers are specific to production of good Z, the unskilled workers are specific to production of goods T and N. Physical capital is, on the other hand, used by all these three sectors. The production structure thus represents a variant of the Gruen- Corden (1970) model: The traded sector T and the non-traded sector N together form a *nugget* displaying Heckscher-Ohlin properties whereas the Z sector employs a specific factor,

[11] Later in Chapter 6 we allow unskilled workers to acquire skill through education and training. Skilled labour force is therefore endogenously determined.

S, and is connected to the nugget by its common use of physical capital, the mobile factor. There is also an imported input (I) used in production of non-tradeables. This is introduced to capture the import-dependent production features in LDCs and will allow us to examine some implications of trade liberalization.

The traded good *T* is a composite good with all tradeables, other than *Z*, lumped together. This composite serves to aggregate a number of different commodities consumed at home but produced abroad, whereas it also contains the single traded commodity (other than *Z*) produced at home. Domestic markets for these goods and that of non-tradeables are perfectly competitive. Input coefficients are fixed and factor prices are flexible. The price of non-tradeables is flexible and adjusts to clear any excess demand for or supply of non-tradeables. By contrast, trade allows consumption and production of good *T* to differ, with overall trade balanced with the intermediate good imports and the exports of *Z*.

The tradeable, *Z*, is a quality-differentiated search good. Thus its quality is observable to all prior to consumption and is indexed by $Q \in [0, 1]$ [12]. This quality-differentiated good is not, however, domestically consumed but is produced entirely for the export market. We call this good a non-traditional export to distinguish it from the (homogeneous) tradeable, T, which we call the traditional traded good. For any given quality of non-traditional exports, skilled labour and capital are used in fixed proportions in production. But the production technology is such that higher quality varieties are more intensive in capital relative to lower quality varieties. In addition we have diminishing returns to capital (with respect to quality). The production technology is summarized in terms of the following input coefficients:

$$a_{KZ} = a_{KZ}(Q),\ a_{KZ}(0) > 0,\ a'_{KZ}(Q) > 0,\ a''_{KZ}(Q) > 0 \tag{4.1}$$

The skilled labour coefficient, a_{SZ}, is invariant for different qualities. This is a simplifying assumption. With fixed coefficients and with a fixed endowment of skilled labour specific to this sector, the output of *Z* becomes fixed irrespective of quality. These assumptions allow us to focus on the quality dimension of *Z* instead of the quantity dimension.

[12] By making quality observable to all we essentially rule out the problem of informational externality.

Since the non-traditional export good is not domestically consumed, what matters to producers in choosing the best quality is the price of exports available in world markets. Of course there is a rising price schedule, $P_Z^*(Q)$, because consumers in the world market are willing to pay more for higher quality items. Regarding the shape of the $P_Z^*(Q)$ schedule we assume:

$$P_Z^* = P_Z^*(Q),\ P_Z^{*'}(Q) > 0,\ ra''_{KZ}(Q) > P_Z^{*''}(Q) > 0 \qquad (4.2)$$

The restriction on the curvature of the $P_Z^*(Q)$ schedule is analogous to the condition derived in Chapter 3 for ensuring an interior solution.

The exchange rate is assumed to be fixed and set at unity, allowing world prices to be quoted in domestic currency units. Given the production technology and foreign tastes summarized in (4.1) and (4.2) respectively, profit maximization leads to the following marginal condition:

$$P_Z^{*'} = ra'_{KZ}(Q) \qquad (4.3)$$

where, r is the rate of return to capital faced by producers. Marginal revenue from quality of exports, $P_Z^{*'}$, must be equal to marginal cost of the same, $ra'_{KZ}(Q)$. For any given rate of return to capital, this marginal condition indicates how exporters choose product quality and is illustrated in Figure 4.1. The upward sloping concave curve, $C_Z(w_S^o, r_o)$, represents the unit cost of producing different qualities for a given set of factor prices. Any change in skilled wage shifts this curve without affecting the slope. By contrast, any change in the return to capital affects the curve's slope as well as its position. Given such a cost curve and the price-quality schedule, $P_Z^*(Q)$, producers choose the quality Q_0 corresponding to the tangency point A_0 where the marginal condition is satisfied. The assumed ranking of second derivatives in (4.2) ensures that an interior tangency such as at A_0 in Figure 4.1 does indeed represent an optimal position. Thus small changes in (foreign) tastes or (policy-induced) changes in the return to capital produce small changes in quality.

Choosing quality optimally implies a relationship between quality and the return to capital. Consider, for example, an increase in the return to capital from r_o to r_1, due to some disturbance in the rest of the economy. This increases the marginal cost for any given quality. Since quality enhancement raises costs further and faster than the world price as indicated in (4.1) and (4.2), profit is now maximized at a lower quality. In Figure 4.1, the $C_Z(w_S, r)$ curve would shift up and become steeper. If entry and exit are unrestricted, competitive forces will drive down the skilled wage until the new steeper curve $C_Z(w_S^1, r^1)$ is tangent to the price-quality schedule at a point like A_1. This inverse relationship is shown in Figure 4.2 by the curve labeled π_Z.

Formally, such a relationship can be obtained by differentiating the marginal condition (4.3):

$$\frac{dr}{dQ} = -\frac{r a''_{KZ}(Q) - P_Z^{*''}}{a'_{KZ}(Q)} < 0 \tag{4.4}$$

But this π_Z curve only indicates what quality is chosen by producers when they face a particular price of capital. But it does not tell by itself what the *equilibrium* quality will be because the rate of return to capital is yet to be determined. For this we need another relationship between return to capital and quality and the market clearing condition for non-tradeables provides such a relationship to complete the specification of equilibrium:

$$D_N(p, y) = X_N \tag{4.5}$$

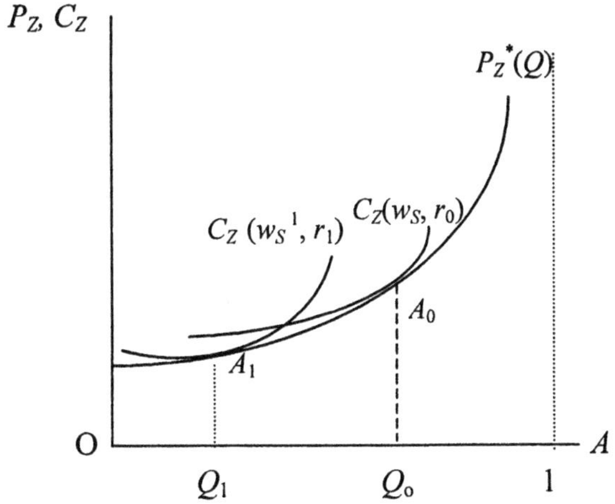

Figure 4.1: Quality Selection for a Given Set of Factor Prices

where $p = P_N / P_T$ denotes the relative price of non-tradeables (compared with traded goods consumed locally) and y denotes domestic real income. The budget constraint assumed to underlie the demand function implies that market-clearing condition for non-tradeables also ensures that overall trade is balanced[13].

Output levels of non-tradeables and traditional tradeables are determined from the full employment conditions for capital and unskilled labour:

$$a_{LT}X_T + a_{LN}X_N = \overline{L} \tag{4.6}$$

$$a_{KT}X_T + a_{KN}X_N = K^*(Q) \tag{4.7}$$

where, $K^*(Q) = \overline{K} - a_{KZ}(Q)X_Z$ denotes the (net) capital stock available for the rest of the economy. As already noted, the output of non-traditional exports, X_Z, is determined independently of the level of quality chosen as well as of factor prices because the input coefficient, a_{SZ}, is fixed and the endowment of skilled labour is given:

$$a_{SZ}X_Z = \overline{S} \tag{4.8}$$

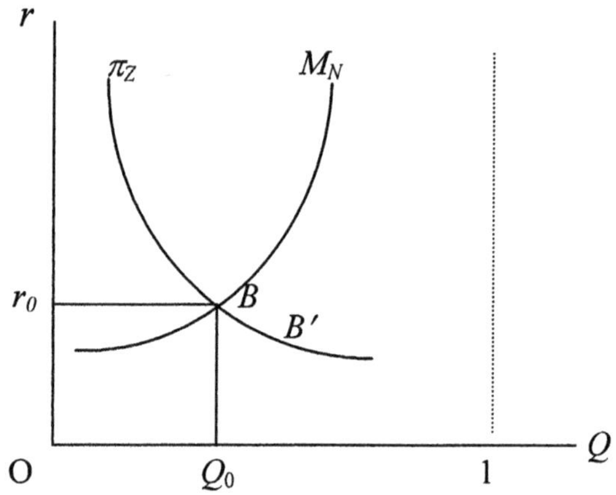

Figure 4.2: Export Quality and Rate of Return to Capital

[13] Real income depends upon the set of world prices, and endowments of capital, unskilled and skilled labour. In what follows it will be clear how change in real income, induced by policy changes, spill over to affect demand for non-tradeables. An explicit solution for real income is avoided to keep things less cumbersome.

Therefore, for any given quality of non-traditional exports, the amount of capital available for the nugget, say $K^*(Q_0)$, together with the endowment of unskilled labour determine the outputs of non-tradeables and traditional tradeables as illustrated by point E_0 in Figure 4.3.

As typically assumed, non-tradeables are posited to be relatively labour intensive compared with tradeables. With quality helping to determine X_N, the relative price of non-tradeables must clear the non-traded market. Finally, the competitive profit conditions determine factor prices:

$$a_{LT}w + a_{KT}r = P_T^* \tag{4.9}$$

$$a_{LN}w + a_{KN}r = P_N - a_{IN}P_I^* \tag{4.10}$$

where, P_I^* is the price of the imported input; a_{IN} is the fixed input coefficient, and P_N is the market-clearing price of non-tradeables.

An increase in the quality of non-traditional exports would reduce capital available for the rest of the economy, which raises the production of non-tradeables by the standard output magnification effect. In the neighbourhood of equilibrium real income is not affected, so that the non-traded market would now clear at a lower price, forcing down the unskilled wage rate and increasing the rate of return to capital. Thus, from the market-clearing condition for the non-traded good what we get is a positive relationship between the quality of the non-traditional exports (Q) and the rate of return to capital (r). Such a relationship is shown by the curve labeled M_N in Figure 4.2. The appendix shows that a reversal of factor intensity ranking for the (T, N) nugget does not affect this positive relationship between r and Q along the M_N curve.

The equilibrium quality of the non-traditional exports, together with the rate of return to capital, is thus determined at the point where the profit maximizing quality is consistent with the non-traded market being cleared. Referring back to Figure 4.2, point B denotes such an equilibrium. Note that the M_N locus is associated with a particular endowment of unskilled labour (or with a particular employment level). Consider, for example, an exogenous increase in the endowment of unskilled labour. Even though this increases real income, the magnification effect in the (T, N) nugget leads to an excess supply of non-tradeables, thereby reducing their prices for any given quality of non-traditional exports.

Consequently, the unskilled wage rate would fall and the return to capital would increase, implying an upward shift of the M_N locus. By contrast, an exogenous fall in the endowment of labour (or in employment levels) would shift the corresponding M_N locus downwards, resulting in a new equilibrium such as point B′ in Figure 4.2.

What emerges from the above analysis is the factor-proportion theory of export quality. A country with relatively smaller endowment of capital (or more unskilled workers) will have a higher rate of return to capital relative to unskilled wage. Consequently it will produce a lower quality variety of exports compared to other economies that are endowed with greater capital stock (or fewer unskilled workers). Since physical stock of capital (relative to other factors) is usually smaller in the developing countries compared to that in the developed countries, the above analysis offers an explanation for quality variations across them[14].

On the other hand, the supply side link between income distribution and export quality implies that direct income redistribution policies as well as

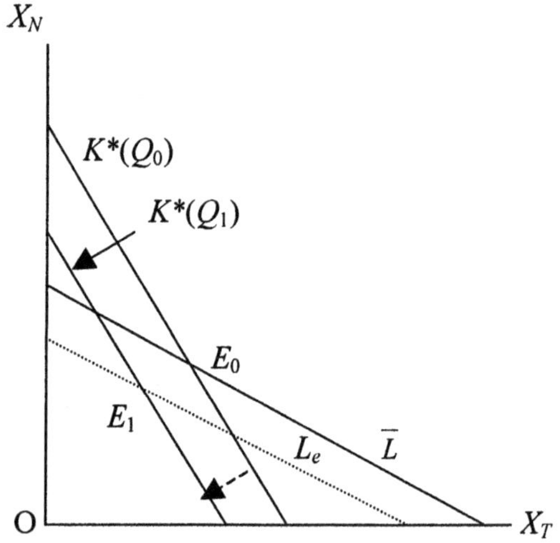

Figure 4.3: Determination of Output Levels

[14] The analysis leaves scope for the technology story as well. If the economy under consideration has a superior technology compared to countries with similar endowment patterns, then it will export a higher quality variety. The technological difference explaining the pattern of trade in quality differentiated good has been more explicitly modeled by Falvey and Kierzkowski (1987).

standard trade policies can be used to improve export quality. At the same time, because the export sector competes with the rest of the economy for scarce capital, quality variations also affect the domestic income distribution. There is, therefore, a two-way causation: (policy-induced) changes in income distribution affect export quality and vice versa.

To analyze each of these aspects in isolation from the other, we examine, first of all, how trade liberalization affects the equilibrium selection of the export quality, and then the implication of a minimum quality standard for the domestic income distribution.

4.3 Trade Policy and Export Quality

With an imported input used in the production of the non-traded good, the simplest way to think of trade liberalization is in terms of a reduction in the ad-valorem tariff on such imports. After all, high input tariffs are typical features of restrictive trade regimes in the LDCs. It is often contended, as elaborated in the earlier chapter, that high input-tariffs force producers to select lower export qualities. Of course, the basic premise that higher export quality requires high-quality foreign inputs is altogether different from what we have in mind here. But the essence of the argument can still be captured because even if the imported input here is not used in production of the quality-differentiated export good, a reduction of tariffs on it does influence the quality choice by affecting the rate of return to capital.

Suppose that, in Figure 4.2, Q_0 indicates an equilibrium with an ad-valorem tariff (t) placed on the imported input. With a reduction in the tariff rate, there will be no shift in the π_Z locus because the imported input is not used in production of non-traditional exports. However, the M_N locus shifts downwards. At the initial level of export quality the reduction in the tariff rate could not influence supply (because the input coefficients are assumed to be fixed) but would raise demand for non-tradeables (and therefore its price) since real incomes experience an increase as the level of tariff distortion is reduced. Such a rise in price of the non-traded good, coupled with the increase in its *effective* price to producers, P_N - $a_{IN}P_I{}^*$, must cause the unskilled wage rate to rise and hence the rate of return to capital to fall. The consequent downward shift in the M_N locus in Figure 4.2 moves the equilibrium to the right resulting in a higher quality level Q_1. Thus, trade liberalization raises the quality level of non-traditional exports.

4.4 Quality Regulation and Income Distribution

Over the last decade quality regulations and standards imposed by the advanced industrialized countries on imports have emerged as the single most important non-tariff barrier on exports of the developing countries. Let us denote such a minimum restriction by $\bar{Q}$. Thus, import of goods from the developing countries with quality levels lower than this minimum standard are not allowed by the importing country. To trace out the distributional consequence of this regulation for the developing country, suppose this is binding for our small open economy in the sense that the initial quality level selected, Q_0, is lower than the minimum standard $\bar{Q}$.

Since higher quality variety of the export good Z is relatively capital intensive, the immediate impact of this quality regulation would be to increase the production of the relatively labour-intensive non-tradeables as some capital would be drawn from the rest-of-the-economy. With the price of non-traded good declining in the process to clear the market, the rate of return to capital would increase and the unskilled money wage would fall. What is to be noted, however, is that this rate of return, say r_1, is greater than the rate at which the quality standard $\bar{Q}$ would have been the *optimal* choice for exporters. Competitive forces in the non-traditional sector drive down skilled wages such that export revenue once again equals the cost of production, but it cannot restore the tangency. That is, for $\bar{Q}$, marginal cost exceeds marginal quality,

$$a'_{KZ}(\bar{Q})r_1 > P_Z^*(\bar{Q}) \tag{4.11}$$

The minimum quality restriction is, therefore, distortionary leading to a loss of real income and hence lower demands for both non-tradeables and traditional traded goods. Since the market for non-tradeables must clear domestically, this necessitates a further fall in the price of non-tradeables and consequently the rate of return to capital increases further. Thus the minimum export quality requirement lowers both the unskilled and the skilled wage rates and redistributes income against workers. How dose it affect the relative position of the unskilled workers vis-à-vis the skilled ones?

A little manipulation of the competitive price condition for the non-traditional export sector yields the change in skilled wage rate following quality enhancement to meet the minimum standard as:

$$\hat{W}_S = \frac{1}{\theta_{SZ}}[\beta - \theta_{KZ}\gamma]\hat{Q} - \frac{\theta_{KZ}}{\theta_{SZ}}\hat{r} \qquad (4.12)$$

where,

$$\beta \equiv \frac{QP_Z^{*'}(Q)}{P_Z^*} \quad \text{and} \quad \gamma \equiv \frac{Qa'_{KZ}(Q)}{a_{KZ}}$$

are respectively the quality elasticity of the world price of non-traditional exports and the quality elasticity of capital requirement in production of non-traditional exports.

By (4.11), the term in the parenthesis on the right hand side is non-vanishing and negative. If the domestic exporters could optimally choose their product quality and factor prices could adjust fully, by the marginal condition for optimum this term would have vanished and therefore quality enhancement would have no impact on the skilled wage except through changes in the non-traded price and therefore in the rate of return to capital as captured by the second term in (4.12). But now, quality being enhanced exogenously to a point where the marginal cost of quality is higher than the marginal revenue at the margin, such an enhancement of quality depresses the skilled wage rate further. Subtracting $\hat{w}$ from both sides of (4.12) and using its (inverse) relation with the change in the rate of return to capital, obtained from the competitive price condition for the traditional composite trade good, we arrive at expression for the change in the wage gap:

$$\hat{W}_S - \hat{W} = \frac{1}{\theta_{SZ}}[\beta - \theta_{KZ}\gamma]\hat{Q} - \left[\frac{\theta_{KZ}}{\theta_{SZ}} - \frac{\theta_{KT}}{\theta_{LT}}\right]\hat{r} \qquad (4.13)$$

Since quality enhancement raises the rate of return to capital, the wage gap declines if

$$\frac{\theta_{KZ}}{\theta_{SZ}} > \frac{\theta_{KT}}{\theta_{LT}}$$

4.5 Capital Mobility and Market Diversification

It is understandable that the economy will offer a higher quality if foreign buyers' marginal willingness-to-pay for product quality increases. By similar reasoning we can expect that with access to new export markets with different (marginal) willingness-to-pay for quality, consequent upon multilateral trade liberalization, different qualities will be offered in these export markets[15]. This is precisely what we argued in the previous chapter as well.

But the story is not that simple. With initial full employment of capital, attempt to cater new export markets raise the demand for capital and consequently its price. Such increase in capital cost robs off, in part, incentives offered by the emerging export markets and at the same time makes exports to the existing market unprofitable. Under such circumstances the capital constraint prohibits the small open economy to all the markets. This is not surprising, however. Different qualities essentially involve separate production processes and can be regarded *as if* different goods. Given this interpretation, it is obvious that the number of goods that can be domestically produced is limited by the number of domestic factor of production. Only if all the goods are traded, production of more than one quality can be sustained by meeting domestic demand for some other good entirely through imports. Herein lies the difference between the partial equilibrium analysis of the previous chapter in which input prices and therefore the cost of quality had been considered to be given to the firm, and the general equilibrium analysis in which these variables are essentially endogenous.

What may, however, appear to be surprising is that the economy may well end up not catering the new market where the marginal willingness to pay for quality is higher. That is, a small open economy may not raise its export quality at all with the opening up of new markets. All depends on whether the new market offers higher price than the existing export market for *all* possible qualities. Otherwise the endowment pattern of the country becomes important. Only if it is a capital-abundant country with corresponding rate of return to capital lower than some critical level (to be defined later) or capital-market liberalization depresses the initially high domestic rate of return to capital below such critical rate, the country will cater to the emerging market (which offers higher price only for qualities

[15] Of course, we have in mind segmented export markets.

exceeding some minimum level) with higher export quality. In this section we formalize this argument and provide a justification for capital market liberalization.

Suppose globalization opens up a new market in country-B for the good-Z exported by the small open economy under consideration. Buyers in this emerging market are more sensitive to quality than their counterparts in the existing country-A market. That is,

$$P'_{ZB}(Q) > P'_{ZA}(Q) \quad \forall\ Q \in [\,0,\,1] \tag{4.12}$$

Thus for any given rate of return to capital a higher quality, if at all, will be offered in the country-B market than in the existing country-A market because producers get higher marginal return there for the chosen quality. In terms of Figure 4.4, the π^B-curve (indicating the profit-maximizing qualities for different rates of return to capital when only the country-B market is catered to) lies to the right of the π^A-curve.

But this information is not sufficient to say whether both the markets will be catered and, if not, whether the emerging country-B market will be the one served by a higher quality than before. For this we need to know which market offers higher price for any given quality. There are two possibilities.

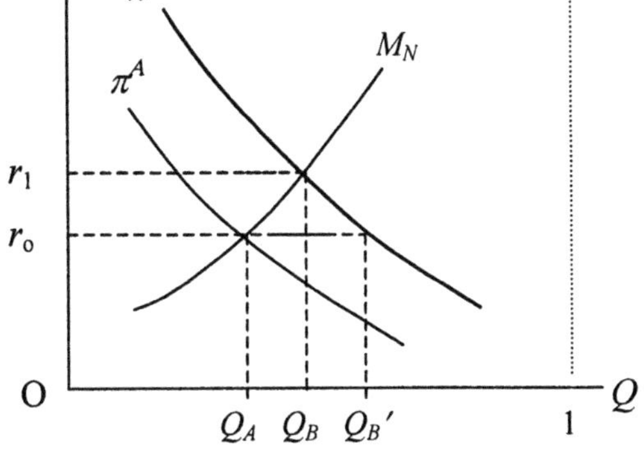

Figure 4.4: Export Qualities in Segmented Markets

Case I:

$$P_{ZB} > P_{ZA} \quad \forall\, Q \in [0, 1] \tag{4.13}$$

Refer to Figure 4.5. Given (4.12) and (4.13), we have drawn the price-quality schedule in emerging country market steeper than and above that in the existing country-A market. Suppose initially the small economy was offering quality Q_A^0 given the equilibrium rate of return to capital as r_0. Once the country-B market opens up for the producers of the small open economy, facing the higher price of good Z there they attempt to cater to this market by offering a higher quality $Q_B^{'}$ with profit (per unit) equal to $BE_B^{'}$. But, additional capital requirement to produce the higher quality raises the return to capital. In Figure 4.5, the unit cost curve shifts up and becomes steeper. Through the competitive mechanism, at the new equilibrium the steeper unit-cost curve must be tangent to the price-quality schedule in market-B.

Two things happen in the process. First, the existing country-A market will no longer be catered as it is now unviable at the new set of factor prices consequent upon the opening up of new market in country-B that offers a higher price. Second, the initial quality enhancement will somewhat be damped through the increase in the rate of return to capital. Thus at the new equilibrium the economy will cater only to the country-B market with a higher quality Q_B. The rate of return to capital will rise and both skilled and unskilled money wages will fall.

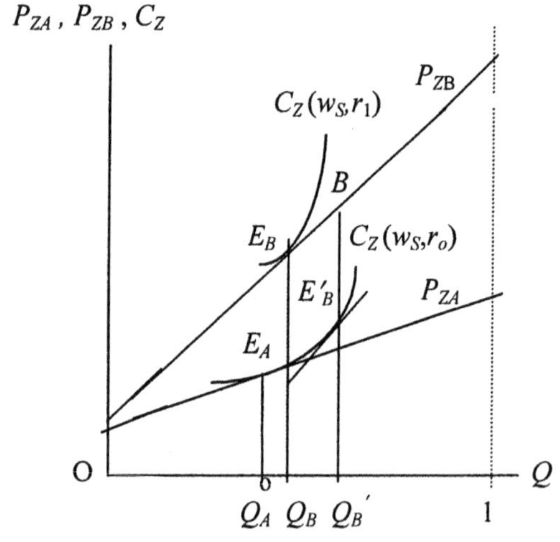

Figure 4.5: Selection of Product Quality

Case II:

$$P_{ZA} > P_{ZB} \quad \forall \quad 0 < Q < \bar{Q} \tag{4.14a}$$

$$P_{ZA} < P_{ZB} \quad \forall \quad \bar{Q} < Q < 1 \tag{4.14b}$$

This is illustrated in Figure 4.6. That is, though the consumers in country-B have higher marginal willingness to pay for quality, they are willing to pay a higher price compared to consumers in country-A only when quality exceeds some critical level $\bar{Q}$. Suppose $\bar{w}_S$ and $\bar{r}$ are the factor prices such that the corresponding unit cost curve is tangent to both the price-quality schedules. For any rate of return to capital greater than $\bar{r}$, only the existing country-A market will be catered whereas for lower rates the new country-B market will be catered. In Figure 4.7 this is indicated by bold discontinuous Π_Z curve.

Therefore, whether the new emerging market with higher marginal willingness to pay will be catered by a small open economy through enhancement of the quality of its export product depends on the initial equilibrium (domestic) rate of return to capital. Consider two small economies, *i* and *j*, with different capital and unskilled labour endowments.

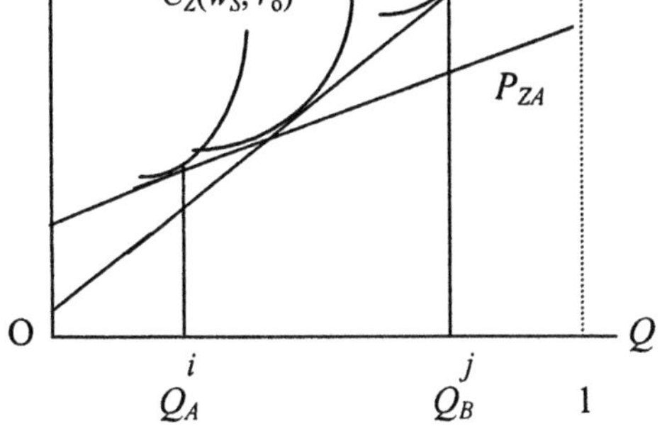

Figure 4.6: Rate of Return to Capital and Selection of Export Market

To fix ideas suppose, ceteris paribus, $L_i > L_j$. As explained in the earlier section, the M_N^i-curve will lie to the left of M_N^j-curve and suppose $r_o^i > \bar{r} > r_o^j$. Thus initially the relatively capital-scarce country-*i* was catering country-A market with lower quality compared to country-*j*. With the opening up of the new country-*B* market, the relatively capital-abundant country-*j* will cater this market by raising its product quality to Q_B^j whereas country-*i* will find it profitable to continue selling in the country-A market with Q_A^j.

The above discussion indicates that in presence of a non-traded good, a small open economy can serve only one of the many export markets with different price-quality schedule. This is because the domestic resource constraint raises the resource costs whenever the country attempts to cater to the emerging markets where the marginal willingness-to-pay for quality is higher in the sense defined in (4.13). Consequently all but one market becomes unprofitable. However, whether the market with higher marginal willingness-to-pay is the one that emerges to be the only profitable market inducing the country to switch to it by enhancing quality of its export good or not, depends on the "average" willingness-to-pay for quality, $P_{Zi}(Q)$. When the different *segmented* export markets cannot be uniquely ranked according to the average willingness-to-pay (Case II above), the endowment of the factor used intensively in higher-quality varieties (here capital) determines the particular market to be catered and the level of quality to be offered.

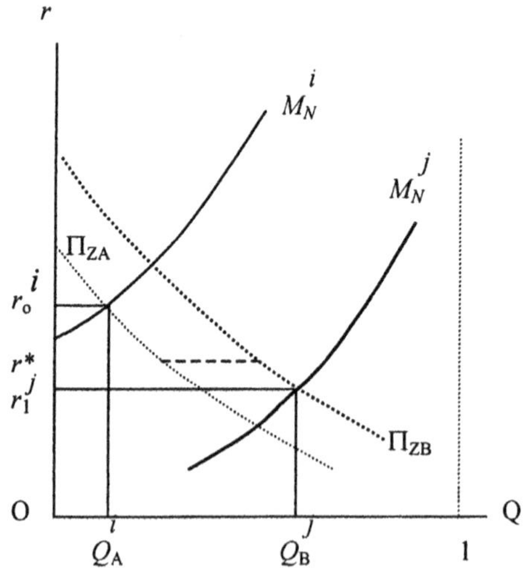

Figure 4.7: Critical Rate of Return to Capital and Selection of Export Market

Does capital-market liberalization help the country in any way? The outcome that the production of the non-traded good allows it to cater to only one export market is unaffected by the capital market liberalization as long as some other scarce factor, here skilled labour, is required to produce the export good. Even though higher quality may not require intensive use of such a factor, as long as expansion of physical production raises its price, both the export markets cannot be catered. But capital market liberalization does help the capital-scarce country to switch to the new market with higher marginal willingness-to-pay (in Case II) and raise the quality of its exports in the process.

This is immediate from Figure 4.7. If the rate of return to capital ruling in the world market is lower than r^* (such as r_1^j), the capital-scarce country-i with $r = r_0^i$ initially, will find it profitable to cater to market-B and offer a higher quality.

4.6 Conclusion

The essence of the argument presented here is that poor quality of exports of a developing country can be an outcome of scarcity of capital. Relative scarcity of capital makes the marginal cost of quality enhancement higher. This induces the producers to select a lower quality.

There is, however, a two-way causation between choice of export quality and factor prices. Due to such two-way causation, whereas a reduction of input tariff improves the quality of exports by lowering the cost of capital, enhancement of quality to meet minimum quality standards lowers both unskilled and skilled wages. This reveals a trade-off between higher export quality and wage inequality when non-traditional exports are less capital intensive than traditional exports.

The binding capital constraint on the export quality imply that allowing domestic producers to borrow capital from abroad at a lower cost, however, frees the economy from the shackles of rising domestic capital cost and enables it to raise export quality. This also makes it possible for the economy to cater to the new emerging export markets where buyers are more sensitive to higher quality. In a world with balanced trade, it may not matter which export market a country serves. But this explains why small countries are not too often observed to produce exports of diversified qualities and sometimes are unable to cater new markets with higher MWP for quality in a regime that restricts foreign capital inflow.

The framework used here, being a full-employment, balanced-trade model, does not fully capture the trade balance and/or employment implications of higher export quality. But it can be extended to create scope for such analyses as well. Of course, one simple way to do so is to introduce money wage rigidity (that fits well with the reality in developing countries) and allow for non-traded market to adjust by itself with consequent employment changes (though with balanced trade) following increase in export quality. This is the primary focus of the next chapter.

5 Wage Policy, Standards and the Labour Market

5.1 Introduction

The general equilibrium analysis of export quality presented in Chapter 4 and its supply side dependence on income distribution reveals that a high-wage economy will usually be a producer of higher quality exports. More precisely, if the unskilled money wage is institutionally set at a level higher than the market-clearing level, the quality of exports will improve. This implication of higher institutionally fixed money wage is quite consistent with most of the European countries.

An important lesson emerges from such a relationship for the developing countries. A flexible wage policy adopted in many of these countries including India during the phase of liberalization and structural reforms in the nineties, should result in lower export quality unless the marginal cost of quality is lowered through innovation and/or capital accumulation[16]. A high-wage policy, therefore, induces higher export quality. Of course, with institutionally set wages higher than the market clearing levels still prevalent in some of the developing countries, the question that remains to be answered is why they cannot often produce export qualities comparable to the European standards. There are two plausible answers to this. First, the level of fixed money wage may still be lower in the developing countries. Second, even in cases where the wages are matched with those in the European countries, quality differences persist because of technological differences.

However, higher institutionally set money wage inflicts a cost upon the society and this limits the scope of such a policy to raise export quality. This is in terms of the loss of employment that such a policy leads to. A high-wage policy raises (lowers) the price of the non-traded good and therefore lowers (raises) its production if it is relatively labour-intensive (capital-intensive) compared to the traditional traded good. Aggregate employment declines as a consequence. There is thus a trade-off between

---

[16] Of course, in the long run when the supply of unskilled workers grow as well, the rate of capital accumulation must be sufficiently high to outweigh the adverse effect of such increase in supply of unskilled workers on the rate of return to capital.

higher export quality achieved through a wage policy and the level of aggregate employment. Any further quality enhancement induced by minimum quality standards in such a situation of institutionally fixed unskilled money wage aggravates the situation by lowering aggregate employment further. This chapter elaborates upon such conflict of policies and targets and the dilemma that the policy makers in the developing countries face.

One way to achieve a higher export quality without inflicting upon any employment loss is to adopt selective wage policy whereby the minimum wage restriction is applied to only certain sectors of the economy and allowing the wage to vary in other sectors. But desirability of such selective minimum-wage policy depends on how does quality enhancement through minimum quality standards change the unskilled money wage in the unregulated sectors. If adjustments in production and changes in composition of output to maintain full employment necessitate a fall in the unskilled money wage, the selective (or sector-specific) minimum-wage policy loses much of its appeal. After all, most of poor in the developing countries are unskilled workers. Of course, work for all unskilled workers can be ensured through such a selective wage policy, which should lower the incidence of poverty. But, if in the process, the unskilled money wage itself falls, those who were previously employed get poorer.

However, as I shall argue later in this chapter, by carefully selecting the sectors where the minimum-wage policy is to be applied, the governments can in fact ensure that the unskilled workers as a whole do not lose in absolute as well as in real terms. A selective minimum-wage policy aimed at achieving the target export quality can, therefore, be made a pro-labour policy.

A similar result has been obtained by Marjit (2000) in a standard Heckscher-Ohlin model with two traded goods where he has shown that a reduction of subsidy level in the regulated sector and consequent reallocation of factors of production towards the unregulated sector raises the unskilled wage there provided, of course, capital is freely mobile and moves out of the regulated sector as well in consequence. There are, however, two major departures of the present analysis. First, sectoral reallocation of factors of production and changes in the composition of output are brought about not by changes in the technique of production but by change in the price of the non-traded good and consequently its other goods, cause a supply shock in the market for non-traded good. This changes its price and the unskilled money wage in the unregulated sectors further. This secondary effect is crucial. Depending on the factor intensity ranking of the regulated and unregulated sectors, this effect either mitigates or reinforces the initial increase in the unskilled wage in the unregulated sector.

5.2 Minimum Wage, Quality Standards and Employment

Consider the same framework as developed in section 4.2 except that the unskilled money wage is pegged at a level $\overline{W}$ higher than the level consistent with the full employment equilibrium depicted in Figures 4.2 and 4.3. At the stroke of the pen such higher money wage lowers the rate of return to capital through the competitive forces given the price of the traditional composite traded good (see eq. 4.9). Let this lower rate of return to capital be r^*. The consequent lower marginal cost of producing higher qualities induces the exporters to raise the product quality to Q^* along the Π_Z locus in Figure 5.1.

With the unskilled money wage pegged institutionally and consequently the rate of return to capital being determined by the world price of the traditional traded good, the price of the non-traded good no longer depends on the domestic demand but is solely determined by cost of production (see eq. (4.10)). Since the non-traded good is relatively labour intensive, the higher minimum unskilled wage raises its price and therefore lowers its demand. There is also the adverse real income effect on demand. The fall

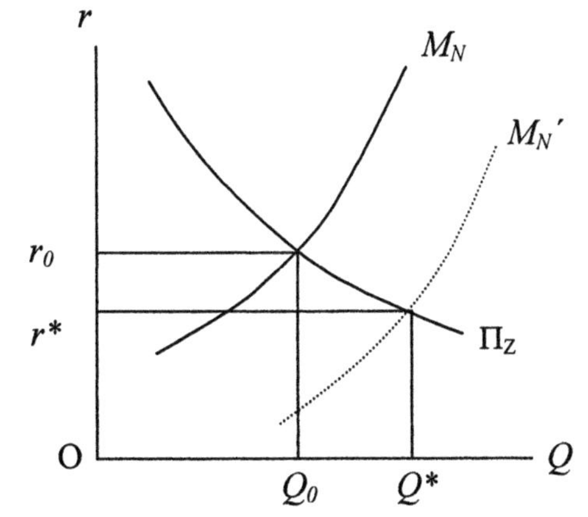

Figure 5.1: Minimum Wage and Export Quality

in aggregate employment due to the price effect (as shown by the point E′ along the $K(Q_0)$ line in Figure 5.2) lowers the real income and therefore the demand for non-traded good further, provided of course, it is a normal good. Demand and aggregate employment thus fall by multiplier effect[17].

On top of these adverse price and real income effects, the output of the non-traded good falls lowering aggregate employment even further due to withdrawal of capital from the *T-N* nugget to sustain the production of the higher quality Q^* of the non-traditional export good *Z*. In Figure 5.2 this is shown by the broken line $K(Q^*)$. By the output magnification or Rybczynski effect such fall in the availability of capital for the production of the traditional traded good and the non-traded good lowers the output of the non-traded good more than the proportionately. All these three effects – the price effect and the real income effect operating on the demand side, and the output magnification effect operating on the supply side – combine together to push the equilibrium at a point E* with p_N^* and y^* being the relative price of the non-traded good and the real income respectively consistent with such an unemployment equilibrium. Referring back to Figure 5.1, the emerging unemployment shifts the M_N curve to $M_N^{'}$.

What follows from the above inter-relationship between unskilled money wage, export quality and aggregate employment, is that starting from an initial situation of minimum wage, a flexible wage policy or lowering of the minimum wage though raises aggregate employment, loses much of its appeal when the degradation of export quality is taken into account. On the other hand, there is a limit to which the export quality can be raised by a small open economy through the wage policy. It depends on the level of employment that it is willing to trade-off.

It is obvious by now that any attempt to raise product quality through minimum quality standards will lead to further employment loss in face of a minimum wage policy. This works via the output magnification and induced real income effects. Thus, with prevalence of money wage rigidity in most of the developing countries, the quality regulations imposed by the advanced industrialized importing countries will put an excess burden on them in the form of loss of employment and real income.

How does a tariff reduction affect the export quality and the aggregate employment under these circumstances? As long as the imported input is

---

[17] The same adverse effect would have arisen had the non-traded good been relatively labour intensive.

used in the non-traded sector, reduction of input tariff will not affect the export quality. What remains is just the employment effect. The lower price of the non-traded good now raises its demand and therefore its output. Of course, the output of the traditional traded good contracts because the capital stock available for these sectors remains the same. But aggregate employment increases since the non-traded good is relatively labour intensive.

On the other hand, if the imported input is used only in the sector that produces the traditional traded good *T*, export quality falls as a consequence of a reduction in the input tariff. This is because, with the effective (world) price of the traditional traded good rising as the input tariff is slashed, the rate of return to capital and therefore the marginal cost of quality rises. Thus, with money wage rigidity, input tariff reduction can no longer raise export quality. Moreover, whether such a policy favourably or adversely affects the aggregate employment depends on the production structure of the nugget.

5.3 Selective Wage Policy

An alternative policy option for the government to achieve the target level of export quality is selective, rather than uniform minimum wage policy: Peg the unskilled money wage in any one of the sectors comprising the

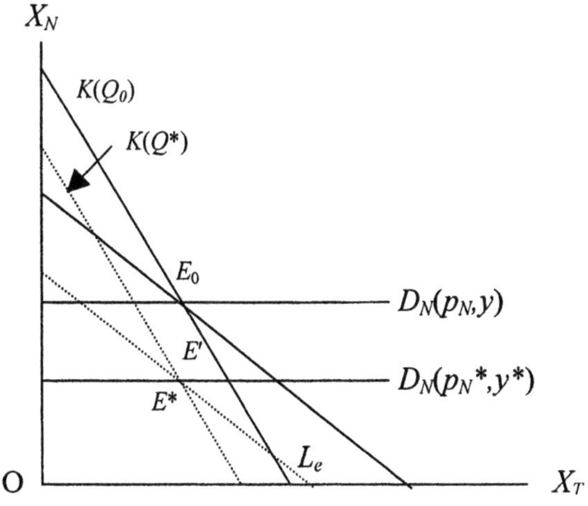

Figure 5.2: Unemployment in the T-N Nugget

nugget and allow the unskilled money wage in rest of the economy to be determined by the interplay of demand for and supply of unskilled labour. With such a policy we need not be worried about raising export quality at the cost of aggregate employment. The non-traded market is always cleared through changes in the price of the non-traded good thereby absorbing any excess supply of labour whatsoever.

But what is to be concerned about is the direction of change in the money wage rate in the rest of the economy. If the unskilled workers employed in the non-intervened sectors experience a fall in their earnings, this selective minimum-wage policy loses much of its appeal as an instrument of raising export quality. However, as we demonstrate, the direction of the change in the unskilled wage depends on the nature of the sector where the minimum-wage policy is introduced. To focus on this particular issue, we consider minimum-wage policies in the traditional traded sector and in the non-traded sector in turn.

5.3.1 Minimum-Wage Restriction in the Traditional Traded Sector

Let the money wage for the unskilled workers employed in the traditional traded sector is set at a higher level $w_T = \bar{w} > w_o$ where w_o is the money wage rate consistent with the full employment equilibrium described earlier. We distinguish the flexible money wage for unskilled workers employed in the non-traded sector from the pegged rate by denoting the former by w_N.

Given the world price of traditional traded good, competitive profit condition (2) immediately reduces the rate of return to capital:

$$\hat{r} = -\frac{\theta_{LT}}{\theta_{KT}}\hat{w}_T \tag{5.1}$$

where $\hat{w}_T \equiv (\bar{w} - w_o)/\, w_o$. The lower capital cost now induces the exporters to raise product quality. In terms of Figure 5.3, the M_N-curve now becomes horizontal at this lower rate of return to capital and quality increases along the π_Z-curve. Note that, once the w_T is pegged, the rate of return to capital is determined uniquely by the world price of the traditional traded good. Any (policy induced) change in the export quality can no longer produce a change in this return. The entire burden of the resource reallocation effect of different levels of export quality is then borne by the unskilled workers, employed in the non-traded sector at a flexible money wage, and by the skilled workers.

How does the unskilled wage in the non-traded sector change? Much depends on how the non-traded price is affected following the increase in the export quality. At the initial P_N, the fall in the rate of return to capital, consequent upon pegging of the traded-sector money wage at a higher level, raises the money wage in the non-traded sector as is evident from the competitive profit condition [see (4.10) in Chapter 4]. On the other hand, the increase in the export quality consequent upon the fall in the capital cost withdraws capital from the nugget and raises the production of the non-traded good if it is labour-intensive relative to the traditional traded good. For a given real income, the emerging excess supply reduces the price of non-tradeables thereby reducing the money wage rate for those employed in this sector. Therefore, the net change in w_N is ambiguous. Formally[18],

$$\hat{P}_N = \frac{\gamma\lambda_{LT}\lambda_{KZ}}{\varepsilon_N|\lambda|}\hat{Q} \tag{5.2}$$

$$\hat{w}_N = \frac{1}{\theta_{LN}}\left[\frac{\gamma\lambda_{LT}\lambda_{KZ}}{\varepsilon_N|\lambda|}\hat{Q} + \theta_{KN}\frac{\theta_{LT}}{\theta_{KT}}\hat{w}_T\right] \tag{5.3}$$

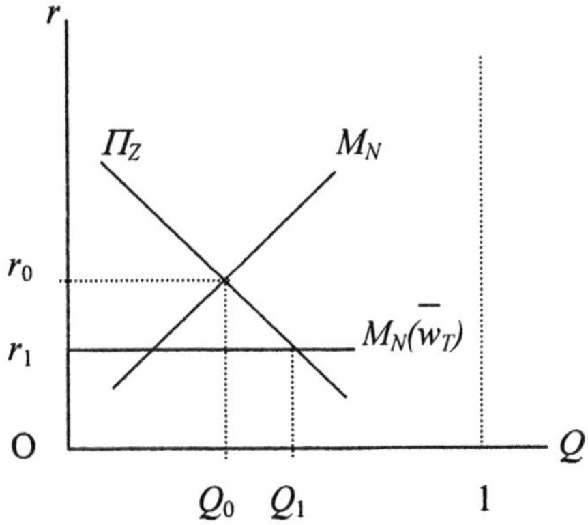

Figure 5.3: Export Quality and Rate of Return to Capital

[18] See appendix.

where, $\gamma \equiv Qa'_{KZ}(Q)/a_{KZ}(Q)$ is the quality-elasticity of capital in production of non-traditional exports, ε_N is the price elasticity of demand for the non-traded good, λ_{ij} and θ_{ij}s ($i = K,L$; $j = 1,2$) are the usual employment and cost shares respectively (with reference to the nugget) and $|\lambda| \equiv \lambda_{LT}\lambda_{KN} - \lambda_{KT}\lambda_{LN}$.

But if the non-traded good is capital intensive relative to traditional traded good, $|\lambda| > 0$, the money wage in the rest of the economy unambiguously increases. It is interesting to know, however, what happens to the real wage in such a case. From the competitive profit condition we get, using (5.2) and (5.3),

$$\hat{w}_N - \hat{P}_N = \frac{\theta_{KN}}{\theta_{LN}}\left(\frac{\gamma\lambda_{LT}\lambda_{KZ}}{\varepsilon_N|\lambda|}\hat{Q} + \frac{\theta_{LT}}{\theta_{KT}}\hat{w}_T\right) \tag{5.4}$$

The unskilled workers in the non-traded sector, therefore, unambiguously gain (given $|\lambda| > 0$):

$$\hat{w}_N > \hat{P}_N > 0 = \hat{P}_T^* \tag{5.5}$$

Their counterparts in the traditional traded sector (the intervened sector), on the other hand, gain in terms of the traded good, $\hat{w}_T > 0 = \hat{P}_T^*$, but may gain or lose in terms of the non-traded good.

5.3.2 Minimum-Wage Restriction in the Non-Traded Sector

Suppose the minimum-wage restriction is applied to the non-traded sector employment, i.e., $w_N = \bar{w} > w_o$, with no such restriction for the employment in the traditional traded sector. Immediately, given the competitive profit condition in the non-traded sector, the rate of return to capital falls which, in turn raises the export quality. But with capital stock already fully employed, the additional capital required to produce the higher quality of the export good (Z) must be drawn from the nugget. The consequent reduction in the availability of capital for the nugget then raises the production of the non-traded good if it is labour intensive relative to the traditional traded good. Under such circumstances, the market for the non-traded good must clear at a lower price, which, in turn, reduces the rate of return to capital given the pegged unskilled money wage. Hence, the initial fall in the rate of return to capital gets reinforced if the non-traded good is relatively labour intensive, i.e., $|\lambda| < 0$ (see appendix):

$$\hat{r} = -\left[\frac{\theta_{LN}}{\theta_{KN}}\left\{1+\frac{\beta\gamma\lambda_{LT}\lambda_{KZ}}{\alpha\varepsilon_N\theta_{KN}|\lambda|}\right\}\right]\hat{w}_N \tag{5.6}$$

where, $\hat{w}_N \equiv (\overline{w} - w_o)/\, w_o$, $\beta \equiv ra'_{KZ}(Q), \alpha \equiv Q\left[P_Z^{*''}(Q) - ra''_{KZ}(Q)\right] < 0$.

Note that with this type of selective wage policy that pegs the unskilled money wage in the non-traded sector, the M_N-curve is negatively (positively) sloped if the non-traded good is relatively labour (capital) intensive. Thus, in Figure 5.4, the downward sloping M_N-curve shifts down as the rate of return falls to r'_o (say) at the initial export quality Q_o, consequent upon pegging the w_N at a higher level. Producers of the non-traditional export good respond to this lower capital cost by raising product quality along the π_Z-curve which reduces rate of return to capital further to r_1[19].

On the other hand, if the non-traded good is capital intensive relative to traditional traded good, $|\lambda| > 0$, its price and consequently the rate of return to capital increase due to the increase in export quality. However, the initial fall in the rate of return to capital only gets dampened (see Figure 5.5).

In any case, therefore, the rate of return to capital falls consequent upon pegging of w_N. Accordingly, competitive profit condition in the traditional traded sector drive up the money wage for the unskilled workers employed in this sector irrespective of any factor intensity condition.

Regarding the change in the real wage we observe that as long as the non-traded good is relatively labour intensive, unskilled workers gain unambiguously with those employed in the traditional traded sector (the non-intervened sector) experiencing relatively larger gain (see appendix):

$$\hat{w}_T > \hat{w}_N > 0 = \hat{P}_T^* > \hat{P}_N \tag{5.7}$$

---

[19] The M_N-curve is drawn flatter than the π_Z-curve to ensure stability of equilibrium.

Otherwise, change in the real wage following the selective minimum-wage policy is ambiguous.

5.3.3 Choice of Selective Minimum-Wage Policy

From the above discussions it appears that regardless of the factor intensity condition the minimum wage restriction for unskilled workers employed in the non-traded sector raises the money wage for workers employed in the rest of the economy. Moreover, there are the real wage gains for all unskilled workers irrespective of in which sector they are employed if the non-traded good is relatively labour intensive. On the other hand, in case the minimum-wage restriction is applied to the traditional traded sector, the unskilled money wage in the rest of the economy increases only if non-tradeables are capital intensive. These results can be summarized in the following two propositions:

Proposition 5.1:

a) A sector-specific minimum wage policy raises the quality of exports and maintains full employment regardless of the sector in which it is applied.
b) If the minimum wage is applied to the relatively labour-intensive sector, be it the sector producing the traditional traded good or the non-traded good, the unskilled money wage in the unregulated sector increases and is in fact higher than the regulated wage.

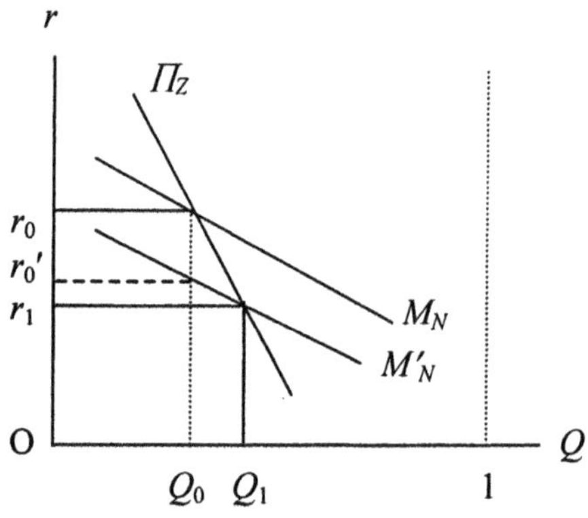

Figure 5.4: Minimum Wage in Labour Intensive Non-traded Sector

Proposition 5.2:

The real wage of the unskilled workers increases regardless of where they are employed if the non-traded sector is regulated and it is relatively labour intensive.

Since usually the non-tradeables are labour intensive relative to traded goods, from these two propositions it follows that the minimum-wage restriction applied to the non-traded sector, instead to the traded sector, is the desirable policy option to achieve the target level of export quality. Such a policy ensures not only money wage gains but also real wage gains for all unskilled workers.

5.4 Conclusion

A small open economy can attain a target export quality which is acceptable in the importing country through a pro-labour income redistribution policy. Minimum wage restriction all around can certainly raise export quality to the desired level, but only at the cost of unemployment. But a selective minimum wage policy whereby the money wage of unskilled workers is pegged only in certain sectors of the economy might actually benefit unskilled workers employed in other sectors and yet raise the export quality. More precisely, if the non-traded good is labour intensive relative to the composite traded good, pegging the money wage in the non-traded sector ensures both the money and the real wage gains for all unskilled workers.

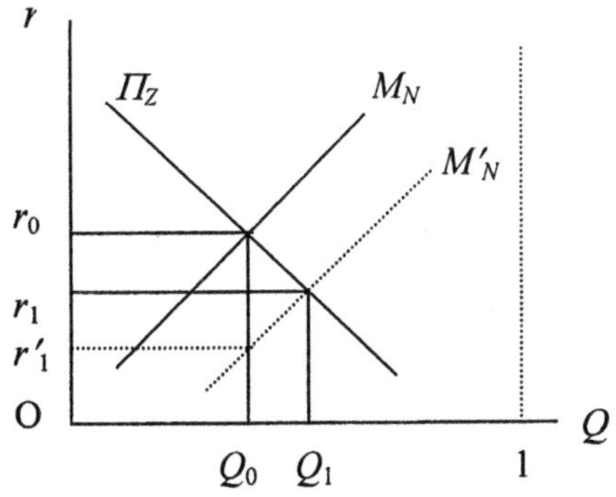

Figure 5.5: Minimum Wage in Capital Intensive Non-Traded Sector

Appendix

I. Export Quality and Price of the Non-Traded Good

Consider the percentage change forms of the labour and the capital constraints:

$$\lambda_{LT}\hat{X}_T + \lambda_{LN}\hat{X}_N = 0 \tag{A.1}$$

$$\lambda_{KT}\hat{X}_T + \lambda_{KN}\hat{X}_N = -\gamma\lambda_{KZ}\hat{Q} \tag{A.2}$$

where, γ is the quality-elasticity of capital in production of good-Z.

These two equations solve for the change in production of the non-traded good:

$$\hat{X}_N = -\frac{\gamma\lambda_{LT}\lambda_{KZ}}{|\lambda|}\hat{Q} \tag{A.3}$$

Then using the market clearing condition we arrive at the change in price of the non-traded good.

II. Real Wage in the Unregulated Non-Traded Sector

By the zero-profit condition in the non-trade sector, the change in real wage for workers employed in the unregulated non-traded sector, when measured in terms of the non-traded good, equals:

$$\hat{w}_N - \hat{P}_N = \left[\frac{1}{\theta_{LN}}\hat{P}_N - \frac{\theta_{KN}}{\theta_{LN}}\hat{r}\right] - \hat{P}_N \tag{A.4}$$

Using (5.1), this boils down to (5.4) in the text.

III. Minimum Wage in the Non-Traded Sector and Factor Returns

Note that, now the change in wage for unskilled workers employed in this sector is (exogenously) determined by the extent to which their money wage is pegged at a level higher than the market clearing one. From the zero-profit condition in the non-traded sector it follows that such a pegging of the money wage lowers the rate of return to capital at the rate equal to,

$$\hat{r} = \frac{1}{\theta_{KN}} \hat{P}_N - \frac{\theta_{LN}}{\theta_{KN}} \hat{w}_N \tag{A.5}$$

Of course, this change in the rate of return incorporates the effect of change in price of the non-traded good as well which is induced by such pegging of the unskilled money wage.

From the marginal condition for selection of quality (see eq. (4.3)), on the other hand, it follows that,

$$\hat{Q} = \frac{\beta}{\alpha} \hat{r} \tag{A.6}$$

where, β and α are as defined in the text.

Thus, combining (5.2) in the text and (A.6) above we arrive at the change in price of the non-traded good following the pegging of unskilled money wage in this sector at a higher level as:

$$\hat{P}_N = \frac{\beta \gamma \lambda_{LT} \lambda_{KZ}}{\alpha \varepsilon_N |\lambda|} \hat{r} \tag{A.7}$$

Substitution of (A.7) in (A.5) then yields the change in the rate of return to capital as defined in eq. (5.6) in the text.

On the other hand, from the zero-profit condition in the composite traded sector, the change in the money wage for unskilled workers employed there can be obtained as,

$$\hat{w}_T = -\frac{\theta_{KT}}{\theta_{LT}} \hat{r} \tag{A.8}$$

which upon substitution of (5.6) boils down to,

$$\hat{w}_T = \frac{\theta_{LN} \theta_{KT}}{\theta_{KN} \theta_{LT}} \left[1 + \frac{\beta \gamma \lambda_{LT} \lambda_{KZ}}{\alpha \varepsilon \theta_{KN} |\lambda|} \right] \hat{w}_N \tag{A.9}$$

Now, note that since the rate of return to capital must fall at the new equilibrium (as evident from Figures 5.2 and 5.3), it is immediate from (5.6) that the term in the parenthesis on the right hand side in (A.9) is positive regardless of the factor intensity condition. Thus,

$$\hat{w}_T > 0 \tag{A.10}$$

If, however, the non-traded good is relatively labour intensive, i.e., $|\lambda| < 0$, price of the non-traded good must fall since $\alpha < 0$ (see eq. (A.7)). Also since $|\lambda| < 0 \Rightarrow \theta_{KT}\theta_{LN} > \theta_{LT}\theta_{KN}$, so

$$\frac{\theta_{LN}\theta_{KT}}{\theta_{KN}\theta_{LT}}\left[1+\frac{\beta\gamma\lambda_{LT}\lambda_{KZ}}{\alpha\varepsilon\theta_{KN}|\lambda|}\right] > 1$$

Therefore,

$$\hat{w}_T > \hat{w}_N > 0 \tag{A.11}$$

Combining all these we arrive at the price magnification effect of pegging of the unskilled money wage in the non-traded sector as defined in (5.7) in the text.

6 Inter-Linkage Between Skill Formation and Export Quality

6.1 Introduction

The analyses of earlier chapters were essentially short run because export quality was selected for given endowments of skilled and unskilled workers. But the composition and division of the aggregate workforce (measured in physical unit) into skilled and unskilled workers are themselves endogenous variables, at least in the long run, through skill formation. In fact, to the extent to which different qualities of the non-traditional export good use skilled labour in different proportions along with physical capital, the skill formation process and, therefore, the composition of the workforce, is affected by the selection and enhancement of the export quality. Of course, for a given stock of physical capital, a change in the composition of the workforce through skill formation changes factor returns which in turn affects the selection of export quality. There is thus a two-way causation between the choice of export quality by firms and the decision of unskilled workers to acquire skills.

This chapter characterizes such a *long run equilibrium* where export quality and the number of unskilled workers acquiring skill are determined simultaneously. We demonstrate that at the equilibrium producers choose a higher quality of exports than at the short run equilibrium when no skill formation takes place (as characterized earlier) and, therefore, the composition of the aggregate workforce is exogenously given. Skill-formation and endogenous supply of skilled workers also significantly change the relationship between an increase in foreign buyers' willingness-to-pay at the margin and the export quality of a small open economy that was perceived earlier.

However, whether the increase in export quality triggered by such a change is reinforced or damped in the final analysis is essentially related to the question how workers move across skill-specific jobs in the process. On the other hand, given a slightly different production structure than employed in the earlier analysis whereby a higher quality of non-traditional export good requires relatively more skilled workers, an exogenous increase in the stock of physical capital lowers export quality though may induce more workers to acquire skills.

In section 6.2 we describe the slightly altered production structure of the basic model and reexamine the choice of quality at the short run equilibrium. Section 6.3 endogenizes the division of the aggregate workforce through skill formation process and its implication for selection of export quality. In section 6.4 we draw implications of two shocks: a change in the stock of physical capital and a change in the foreign buyers' willingness to pay.

6.2 Export Quality and Skilled Wage: Fixed Supply of Skill

We begin with a short run analysis where the small open economy under consideration is endowed with some skilled labour and there is no addition to such workforce through skill formation even if there may be a premium to skill and incentives for the exogenously given unskilled labour force to acquire skills. This is essentially what we have discussed in the earlier Chapters. However, to highlight the inter-linkage between skill formation and selection of export quality in the long run (considered in the next section), we alter the production structure slightly without any loss of generality.

The small open economy under consideration produces the same three goods: A composite traded good (*T*), a non-traded good (*N*), and a quality-differentiated export good (*Z*), which, to simplify, is assumed not to be consumed domestically. But now goods *N* and *Z* have similar production structures in the sense that both are produced by skilled labour (L_S) and domestic capital (*K*), though, of course, used in different (but fixed) proportions[20]. The composite traded good, on the other hand, does not require any skilled labour for its production. Once again we assume fixed proportions of unskilled labour (L_U) and domestic capital in the production of good *T*. All markets are perfectly competitive, factor prices are fully flexible, and technology exhibits constant returns to scale.

The quality range of good *Z* is assumed to be the same as before. However, since we now assume that the higher quality variety of good *Z* is relatively intensive in skilled labour instead of in physical capital so we rewrite eq. (4.1) as:

---

[20] Engineers and technical personnel employed in construction, a major non-traded sector in many developing countries, typify such a production structure.

$$a_{SZ} = a_{SZ}(Q),\ a_{SZ}(0) > 0,\ a'_{SZ}(Q) > 0,\ a''_{SZ}(Q) > 0 \tag{6.1}$$

The unit cost of producing good Z, which is increasing and convex in quality, should similarly be rewritten as:

$$C_Z = a_{SZ}(Q)w_S + a_{KZ}r \tag{6.2}$$

Once again, with the exchange rate fixed at unity, selection of export quality by domestic producers to maximize profits leads to the following marginal condition:

$$P_Z^{*\prime} = a'_{SZ}(Q)\, w_S \tag{6.3}$$

Given this altered production structure, the selection of export quality now depends on the endowment of skilled labour instead of on the endowment of physical capital. This forms the basis of inter-linkage in the long run between skill formation and export quality. It should now be obvious why we have assumed high-quality varieties of good Z being intensive in skilled labour. Of course, the more general production structure which retains the essence of the analyses in Chapter 4 and at the same time creates scope for analyzing the relation between skill formation and selection of export quality is the one where higher quality varieties require greater amounts of both skilled labour and physical capital though in different proportions. However, without any loss of generality we employ the extreme assumption that capital is used in fixed proportions regardless of the quality of good Z.

The inverse relationship between the profit maximizing export quality (Q) and skilled wage (w_S) that emerges from the marginal condition (6.3), illustrated in the Figure 6.1 by the QQ-curve. This together with the positive relationship between skilled wage and export quality consistent with the market-clearing condition for non-traded good (as stated in eq. (4.5)) and the following full employment and zero-profit conditions (restated in light of the altered production structure), labeled as M_N as before, determines the equilibrium export quality and skilled wage for a fixed endowment of skilled workers:

$$a_{LT}X_T = L_U \tag{6.4}$$

$$a_{SZ}(Q)X_Z + a_{SN}X_N = L_S \tag{6.5}$$

$$a_{KZ}X_Z + a_{KN}X_N + a_{KT}X_T = K \tag{6.6}$$

The pair of competitive zero-profit conditions for non-tradeables and quality-differentiated exportable is shown in equations (6.7) and (6.8):

$$a_{SZ}(Q)w_S + a_{KZ}r = P_Z^*(Q) \tag{6.7}$$

$$a_{SN}w_S + a_{KN}r = P_N \tag{6.8}$$

The positive slope of the curve M_N is explained as follows. An increase in export quality, which requires more skilled labour, would shift the full employment locus for skilled labour (as represented by eq. (6.5)) downwards simply because the amount of skilled labour available for *physical* production would be less than before.

If the quality-differentiated export good is intensive in use of skilled labour (relative to capital) compared with non-tradeables, the other commodity in the *Z-N* nugget, output of non-tradeables would increase at given prices (the Rybczynski effect). In order to clear the market for non-tradeables, their price must fall. By competitive profit conditions such a fall must result in a magnified increase in the skilled wage rate. If the intensity ranking in the *Z-N* nugget were reversed, the output of non-tradeables would have been lowered thus raising its price which would once again cause the skilled wage rate to increase. In any case, therefore, the export quality and the skilled wage rate are positively related.

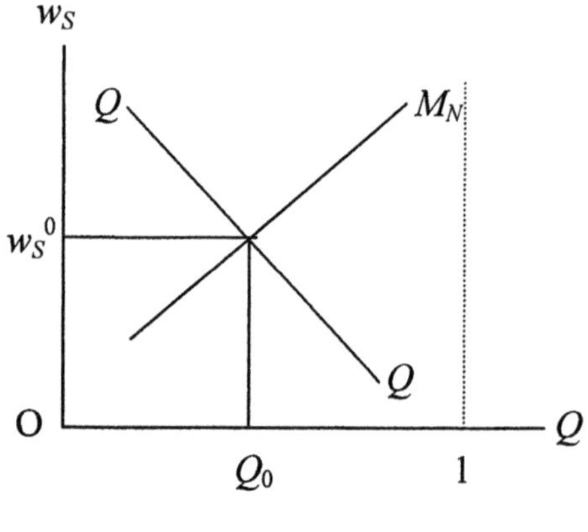

Figure 6.1: Selection of Export Quality

The equilibrium export quality, therefore, corresponds to the intersection of the *QQ* and M_N curves satisfying both the marginal condition (6.3) and the market-clearing condition (4.5).

6.3 Skill Formation and Export Quality: Two-Way Causation

It must now be clear from the above analysis that there is a close link between endowment of skilled labour (or as a matter of fact any other factor endowment) and the selection of export quality through the skilled wage. Any change in the initial endowment of skilled labour either exogenous or through skill formation will affect export quality by changing the skilled wage rate and consequently the marginal cost of quality.

At the same time, selection of a higher export quality by withdrawing some of the scarce skilled labour available for the nugget consisting of the export good and the non-traded good causes the price of the non-traded good to change, leading to changes in factor prices as well. This, as we show below, affects the skill formation decision. There is thus a two-way causation between selection of export quality and skill formation or allocation of a given workforce into skilled and unskilled workers.

6.3.1 The Skill Formation Process

There are many sophisticated models investigating the process whereby skills are formed. We here select a very simple process of skill formation. Findlay and Kierzkowski (1983) considered skill formation simply as a production process whereby an unskilled worker acquires skills by spending some time with one unit of educational input. We here adopt a simplified version of their skill formation process. We make two simplifying assumptions which, of course, do not alter the essence of their argument. First, transformation of one unskilled worker into a skilled one is instantaneous. Time, of course, is an important element in skill formation: The time spent in education determines the level of skills acquired by a worker and therefore the wage that he commands. But such heterogeneity in the level of skills is certainly not what we intend to focus on in this paper. Second, instead of educational input being a type of capital specific to the skill formation process, we assume that such capital is the same type as that required to produce the commodities. But since unskilled workers acquiring skill uses up the educational input, the amount of capital allocated to the skill formation process as educational input can no longer be made available for production of commodities elsewhere once skills are acquired. There is thus an opportunity cost of capital being used as an educational input which is to be borne by unskilled workers willing to acquire skills. These assumptions may appear too naive. However, since our purpose here is not to build up a theory of skill formation but to look into how skill formation and selection of export quality influence each other, we keep things simple as far as possible without, of course, any loss of generality.

The premium to skill, w_S - w, provides the primary incentive for any worker to become skilled. But acquiring skills is not costless. An unskilled worker willing to acquire skills will do so only if the premium to skill is at least as large as the cost of acquiring skill. The costs of acquiring skills, given the above set of assumptions, involve only the cost of training or education. The assumption that each unit of physical capital can either be used as an educational input or be used in production of final goods, coupled with perfect competition and inter-sectoral mobility of factors of production, however, implies that the price per unit that capital commands as educational input must be the same as the market rate of return (r) that it gets when used in production of final goods. With the unit coefficient of educational input in the skill formation process, this means that the cost of acquiring skills for each unskilled workers would just be equal to r. Therefore, an unskilled worker will acquire skills only if,

$$w_S - w \geq r \tag{6.9}$$

The strict equality in (6.9) determines the number of unskilled workers acquiring skills. Note that starting from a situation where $w_S - w > r$, as workers decide to acquire skill, production of non-traded good changes which in turn affects the factor prices. The skill formation process continues until the premium to skill gets equalized with the cost of acquiring skill. Thus, how the production of non-traded good and consequently factor prices change through skill formation holds the centre-stage in determining the equilibrium allocation of workers into skilled and unskilled.

When a worker decides to acquire skills, one unit of capital is withdrawn from the stock of capital for such skill-formation. As the worker gets skilled he makes possible, for any given quality of the export good, additional production of the skill-intensive export good. However, capital is also required for such additional production. Had there been no other use of capital than in production of Z and N, non-traded sector must have contracted to release the required capital. But this is not necessary here because the required capital can be withdrawn from the sector producing the composite traded good. In fact, skill formation does lead to a contraction of this sector [see eq. (6.4)] simply because it implies a fall in the availability of unskilled labour that is specific in this sector. On balance, whether non-traded production should fall or not depends on whether such release of capital from sector-T is sufficient for skill-formation and to sustain the consequent additional production of the export good. Formally, from (6.4) - (6.6) we obtain:

$$\hat{X}_N = \frac{\beta\lambda_{SZ} - \lambda_{KZ}}{|\lambda|}\hat{L}_S + \frac{\gamma_z \lambda_{KZ}\lambda_{SZ}}{|\lambda|}\hat{Q} \qquad (6.10)$$

where,

$$|\lambda| = \lambda_{SZ}\lambda_{KN} - \lambda_{KZ}\lambda_{SN} > 0,\ \beta \equiv \left[\frac{\lambda_{LS}}{\lambda_{LU}}\lambda_{KT} - \lambda_{KS}\right]$$

and γ_Z is the quality-elasticity of the skilled-labour requirement per unit of production of good Z:

$$\gamma_Z = \frac{Qa'_{SZ}(Q)}{a_{SZ}(Q)}$$

λ_{LS} and λ_{LU} are proportions of the workforce (L) that are skilled and unskilled respectively and λ_{KS} is the proportion of capital that is used up in skill formation. The assumption that β is negative, for any given export quality, (6.10) indicates that as more and more unskilled workers acquire skill, the production of non-traded good falls. For a given real income this raises the price of the non-traded good and consequently raises the rate of return to capital. Thus, the cost of acquiring skill increases as more workers acquire skill. This is illustrated in the Figure 6.2 by the *rr*-locus.

On the other hand, both skilled and unskilled wages fall. The change in the premium to skill is, therefore, ambiguous:

$$dw_S - dw = \left[\frac{a_{KT}}{a_{LT}}a_{SZ} - a_{KZ}\right]\frac{dP_N}{|A|} \qquad (6.11)$$

where $|A| = a_{SZ}a_{KN} - a_{KZ}a_{SN} > 0$.

To reduce the multiplicity of cases, suppose the composite traded good is more capital intensive than the quality-differentiated export good in the following sense:

$$\frac{a_{KT}}{a_{LT}} > \frac{a_{KZ}}{a_{SZ}} \tag{6.12}$$

Given (6.12) and that $dP_N/dL > 0$ on the assumption that β is negative, (6.11) indicates that the premium to skill increases as more workers acquire skill. This is indicated by the (w_S - w)-locus in the Figure 6.2 [21]. Thus, workers up to L_0 acquires skill whereas the remaining ($\bar{L}$ - L_0) workers choose to remain unskilled as for them the premium to skill is smaller than the cost involved in acquiring skill[22].

How does the wage-gap, measured by $\hat{w}_S - \hat{w}$, change with such skill-formation? From the zero-profit conditions in the export and composite traded good sectors we get,

$$\hat{w}_S - \hat{w} = \left[\frac{\theta_{KT}}{\theta_{LT}} - \frac{\theta_{KZ}}{\theta_{SZ}}\right]\hat{r} \tag{6.13}$$

Since $\hat{r} > 0$ when skill-formation takes place (see Figure 6.2), so the wage-gap widens if ,

$$\frac{\theta_{KT}}{\theta_{LT}} > \frac{\theta_{KZ}}{\theta_{SZ}}$$

A little manipulation of this condition yields,

---

[21] Stability requires that this schedule be flatter than the *rr* schedule.

[22] Underlying all these adjustments, there is of course the real income change. Note that skill-formation increases money income in general given (6.12): $dY = Kdr + (w_S - w)dL_S + L_S(dw_S - dw) + \bar{L}dw$. Thus, the increase in real income measured in terms of the composite traded good raises the demand for non-traded good and consequently its price reinforcing the initial effects triggered by skill formation.

$$\frac{a_{KT}}{a_{LT}} > \frac{w}{w_S}\frac{a_{KZ}}{a_{SZ}} \tag{6.14}$$

Since $w_S > w$, (6.12) ensures (6.14). Thus, the wage-gap widens despite both the wages falling in consequence of skill-formation.

6.3.2 Selection of Quality under Skill Formation

The above analysis of skill-formation and allocation of a given workforce into skilled and unskilled is incomplete in the sense that such allocation that is consistent with market-clearing condition for the non-traded good is worked out for a *given* export quality. Any other selection of export quality should affect skill-formation by altering the skilled wage. How is the nature of such relationship between change in export quality and skill-formation?

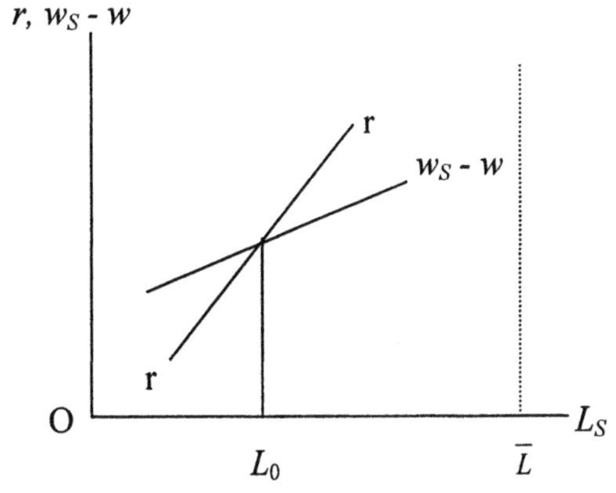

Figure 6.2: Skill Formation Decision

At the initial level of supply of skilled workers, L_0, an increase in export quality implies less skilled labour available for production of the export good and the non-traded good. Since the export good is assumed to be relatively skill-intensive, the production of non-traded good thus increases [see (6.10)], which in turn lowers price of the non-traded good. The rate of return to capital falls and, given (6.12), the premium to skill falls as well in consequence. In Figure 6.2, both the *rr* and w_S - w loci shift down. If the premium to skill falls by a smaller magnitude than the cost of acquiring skill, more unskilled workers decide to acquire skills depending. Thus, the number of skilled workers consistent with market-clearing condition varies positively with the export quality as illustrated in Figure 6.3(a) as Case I.

Figure 6.3(b), on the other hand, illustrates the case where fewer unskilled workers decide to acquire skill as export quality increases and therefore the curve labeled $L_S L_S$ is negatively sloped. This is the case when the skill premium falls by more than the decline in the cost of acquiring skill.

On the other hand, as evident from the discussion in section 6.2, skill-formation affects the choice of export quality as well. In particular, if more workers decide to acquire skill, since the skilled-wage falls as spelled out above (given $\beta < 0$), the producers raise the export quality as evident from the marginal condition (6.3). Thus, we have a positive relationship between number of skilled workers and profit-maximizing export quality as represented by the QQ-curves in Figures 6.3(a) and 6.3(b). The equilibrium export quality, Q_o, and number of skilled workers, L_0, are therefore determined by the intersection of these $L_S L_S$ and QQ curves.

How does this equilibrium export quality compare with the case where the number of skilled workers was determined exogenously? The relevant case is the one where the exogenously given skilled workers, which an economy is endowed with, is less than the number of workers acquiring skill at equilibrium (L_0).

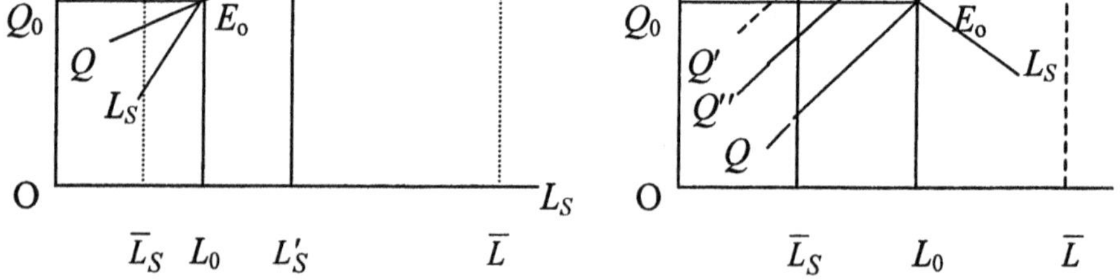

(a): Case I (b): Case II

Figure 6.3: Skill Formation and Export Quality

In such a case, regardless of whether the L_SL_S-curve is positively or negatively sloped, the export quality is better when the supply of skilled labour is endogenously determined through skill-acquiring decision of workers as indicated by the movements along the QQ-curve towards E_0.

In other words, if in the short run equilibrium with exogenously given allocation of the workforce, premium to skill was higher than the cost, some of the unskilled workers decide to acquire skill which serves to lower the skilled wage and consequently raise the export quality. This result is quite consistent with the experience of the economies like India: Higher export quality and world market share is associated with increase in proportion of skilled labour force.

6.4 Foreign Taste Pattern and Supply of Skill

As it appears from the above discussion, increase in the demand for skill-intensive good should have a positive impact on supply of skill in our small open economy. As the new era of globalization has changed the demand pattern and consequently the production specialization across the globe towards the more skill-intensive high-technology goods, we can expect more workers to invest in education and acquire the required skill in the process, provided, of course, such opportunities exist and the skill premium increases relative to the cost of education.

To see whether supply of skill responds positively to such a demand change, suppose the foreign buyers' willingness-to-pay for quality increases at the margin, as reflected in an increase in the world price of good Z. At initial supply of skill and its money wage, such an increase in the world price of good Z serves to raise the export quality since for the domestic producers the marginal revenue increases. This makes less skilled workers available for physical production and output of non-traded good rises [see (6.10)]. The price of non-traded good falls, which in turn lowers the rate of return to capital and with it, given (6.12), falls the premium to skill. Thus, in the above set up the absolute skill premium falls. Supply of skill may still increase since the cost of acquiring skill falls as well. Referring back to Figures 6.3(a) and 6.3(b), the QQ curve shifts up.

When the cost of acquiring skill falls more than the premium, the L_SL_S curve is positively sloped as explained above, and the number of skilled workers increases to L_S' (Figure 6.3(a)). Note that the export quality increases further because the increase in supply of skilled worker lowers the skilled wage by reducing non-traded good production and raising its price. Thus, now the marginal cost of producing the higher quality falls that encourages domestic producers to raise export quality further. If instead, the allocation of a given workforce into skilled and unskilled was exogenous with skill supply fixed at $\overline{L}_S$, an increase in the world price of good *Z* would not have led to this secondary increase in export quality.

But if cost falls less than the premium to skill, as is the case when the L_SL_S curve is negatively sloped (Figure 6.3(b)), does an increase in the world price of good *Z* lower the supply of skill? Certainly not. Note that, since the capital cost incurred during the skill-formation is irrecoverable, i.e., there is no way of de-skilling oneself, such a decision is no longer guided by the change in premium relative to cost unlike the case when an unskilled worker decides about acquiring skill. With increase in the world price of good *Z* and consequent increase in export quality, both the wages increase and, given (6.12), a priori, we can say at most that the premium to skill falls at initial supply of skill. But, of course, it cannot be negative, i.e., the unskilled wage cannot rise above the skilled wage. Thus, there will be no change in the composition of workforce into skilled and unskilled. The L_SL_S curve becomes vertical at L_0. But since the skilled wage increases even at this level of supply of skill, thereby raising the marginal cost of export quality, the initial increase in export quality cannot be sustained. This is shown by the downward shift of the *QQ* curve in Figure 6.4. If the system is stable, such fall cannot be large enough to outweigh the initial increase in export quality. The new equilibrium occurs at a point like E'.

In sum, skill-formation and endogenous supply of skilled workers change significantly the relationship between increase in foreign buyers' willingness-to-pay at the margin and the export quality of a small open economy that was perceived earlier in Acharyya and Jones (2001). Whether the increase in export quality triggered by such a change is reinforced or damped in the final analysis is essentially related to the question how workers move across skill-specific jobs in the process.

6.5 Capital Accumulation and Skill Supply

How does a supply shock, such as an exogenous increase in the physical stock of capital, affect the number of workers acquiring skills and the selection of export quality? Note that at initial factor prices, by the output magnification effect, an increase in the stock of physical capital, ceteris paribus, lowers the production of non-traditional export good and raises that of the non-traded good if the former is skill-intensive relative to the latter. The market for the non-traded good thus clears at a lower price and this serves to lower the rate of return to capital and raise the skilled wage rate. Accordingly, by the marginal condition, export quality falls at the initial composition of the workforce. Thus the *QQ* curve shifts down.

On the other hand, by the zero-profit condition for the traditional traded good, the unskilled wage rate increases following the decline in the rate of return to capital. In fact, given (13), it increases more than proportionately relative to the increase in the skilled wage rate. The premium to skill thus declines along with the cost of acquiring skill. Only if the cost of acquiring skill falls more than the decline in the premium to skill, more workers acquire skill, for any given quality, thereby shifting down the L_SL_S curve. At the new equilibrium, supply of skilled labour increases unless the *QQ* curve shifts more than proportionately to cut the L_SL_S curve at its vertical segment. But if the cost of acquiring skill falls less than the premium to skill, there will be no further skill formation. The only impact of an increase in the stock of physical capital then would be to lower the quality of exports.

6.6 Conclusion

We have demonstrated in this Chapter that selection of export quality by exporters and decision to acquire skills by unskilled workers in a small dependant economy are essentially inter-linked. The decision to skill itself has a positive impact on the level of quality of exports. As more workers acquire skills, the skilled wage rate falls through change in the output and price of the non-traded good consequent upon such increase in supply of skilled workers, and therefore raises the export quality through lowering of the marginal cost of producing higher quality varieties. At the same time, enhancement of export quality affects the skill formation process by altering the factor prices and therefore the premium to skill and the cost of acquiring skills.

7 Dirty Exports and Environmental Standards

7.1 North-South Trade and the Environment

Over the last decade or so, environmental issues have occupied a central place in the trade relations between the North and the South. Implementation of the same environmental standards in the North and the South has been the bone of contention in the dialogue between them. Lower environmental regulation or taxes in the South compared to those in the North are often regarded as an unfair basis of comparative advantage of the South in dirty goods. Trade sanctions imposed by the North on the South are therefore justified as protecting the environment from such ecological dumping. But these arguments are not self-enforcing for two reasons. First, environmental standards or taxes may be different even at the social optimum because of differences in income per capita and taste patterns [Copeland and Taylor (1994), Srinivasan and Bhagwati (1995)]. Thus, lower environmental standards in the South should not necessarily be interpreted as a *deliberate* policy option pursued by the Southern governments. Second, the comparative advantage of South in dirty goods should not always be identified with ecological dumping [Rauscher (1992)]. This would be the case only when the South would not have exported dirty goods to the North without taxing the environment. But in many instances of dirty goods, the South has genuine comparative advantage on the basis of factor proportions. Trade sanctions as a policy option for the North against ecological dumping by the South loses much of its justification in such cases.

Even when there are definite instances of ecological dumping and unfair trade by the South, several issues need to be addressed. First, does a trade sanction imposed by the North on South against such ecological dumping correct for the production distortion and environmental degradation in the South? Second, what are the impacts of such trade sanctions on income distribution and aggregate employment in the South, and, therefore, on the Southern welfare? After all, one needs to weigh the gains from environmental improvement in the South, if at all, against the standard trade losses due to such sanctions. Third, are these trade sanctions optimal for the North? In this chapter we address these issues in particular. Of course, if one is concerned only with the environment, and does not attach any weight on the usual gains from trade, albeit on the basis of perverse comparative advantage, through better production and consumption opportunities, these issues become irrelevant. But certainly such is not the basic premise of this chapter.

Section 7.2 discusses optimality of trade sanctions by the North against ecological dumping by the South. In section 7.3 a justification of Northern environmental regulations on Southern exports of dirty good in which the South has a genuine comparative advantage is provided in the context consumption pollution, instead of the usual assumption of production pollution, generated by such goods. Employment implications of such environmental regulations for the South are discussed in section 7.4.

7.2 Ecological Dumping and Optimality of Trade Sanctions

The arguments of unfair trade and ecological dumping are rooted in the assumption of production pollution (or externality). That is, the dirty goods pollute the environment at their production stage. With the social marginal cost being higher that the private marginal cost, an optimal production tax to correct for such pollution in the North makes prices of dirty goods equal to the social marginal cost. But a lower than optimum production tax in the South means prices of dirty goods are below the social marginal costs. If the North and the South are identical in respect of production technologies, factor endowments and tastes, such a lower than optimum production tax in the South establishes a comparative advantage for it in dirty goods. It exports the dirty goods at a price lower than the social marginal cost. The typical response of the Northern countries to such ecological dumping by the Southern countries is to restrict trade through tariff or non-tariff barriers like an environmental standards requiring cleaner technology for production.

To illustrate the case of ecological dumping and policy implications of Northern response to such a practice, consider a good which can be of different varieties or qualities indexed by $A \in [0, \overline{A}]$. Each variety has some impact on the environment. A low quality of the good degrades the environment more than a higher quality. Thus, the index A captures the environmental-quality of the good. The good with best environmental-quality permissible by the present state of technology, $\overline{A}$, is the one which has least adverse effect on the environment. These qualities are observable to all agents in the market including potential buyers.

If consumers care for the environmental degradation, the environmental-quality of this good should affect the utility they derive from consuming the good. The consumers, therefore, should be willing to pay more for the good of better environmental quality. This is not at odds with the reality. Eco-labeling of products has nowadays become a common feature of product attributes. With the growing concern for environmental protection, consumers are also putting positive and increasing weight on such attributes while choosing from amongst the wide range of products in the market. Automobiles, with Euro-I and Euro-II norms, are typical examples. Computer monitors also qualify for such an example. Besides other attributes of a better monitor, we do take into account whether it is more or less radiant compared to other competing brands.

Suppose each consumer buys only one unit of the good. If the utility function, $u(A)$, has the standard properties, following the same logic as in Chapter 3, then we can draw the indifference curves between the environmental-quality and the price of the good for a representative consumers as the upward-sloping concave downward contours in Figure 7.1. Along each such contours, the consumer derives the same net utility, $u(A) - p$.

The available production technology is indicated by the unit cost (of production) curve labeled CC, which increases at an increasing rate with the environmental quality. The curve C^*C^* lying above CC reflects the social cost of producing one unit of the good of different environmental qualities. The two costs differ because private producers do not internalize the environmental damage that this good inflict upon. Of course, such divergences between social and private costs diminish as the environmental quality of the good improves. Formally, if γ measures the level of average environmental damage, i.e., the extent to which social cost exceeds private cost per unit of production of the good, then

$$\gamma = \gamma(A), \gamma'(A) < 0 \;\; \forall \;\; A \in \left[0, \bar{A}\right] \tag{7.1}$$

with $\gamma(\bar{A}) \geq 0$.

At the free market equilibrium, the competitive industry selects the sub-optimal environmental quality A_C lower than the optimal quality A^* that a social planner would have selected. A pollution-content production tax at the rate $\iota = \gamma(A)$ per unit of output corrects the distortion, provided of course the environmental damage function γ can exactly be measurable. In terms of Figure 7.1, C^*C^* now is the relevant (unit) cost curve for private producers, and accordingly they select A^* as their profit-maximizing quality under the pollution-content production tax.

Consider a Northern country with identical production and cost conditions. Once again through the same pollution-content production tax, the Northern government can ensure that the socially optimum environmental quality is selected by its competitive producers. Now consider a situation where the Northern government imposes the optimal tax schedule $\iota = \gamma(A)$, but the Southern government does not impose any tax whatsoever. Southern producers thus offer the sub-optimal quality A_C.

If there is no trade barrier whatsoever and no cost of transporting the good to the Northern country, the same price-quality menu they can serve to the Northern consumers as to the Southern consumers. Since such a menu makes the Northern consumers strictly better off, they buy the imported variety despite availability of the local variety of higher environmental-quality. Northern producers thus lose their market due to Southern government not imposing any pollution tax and, therefore, encouraging ecological dumping by the Southern producers. This has been the basis of the bone of contention between the North and the South.

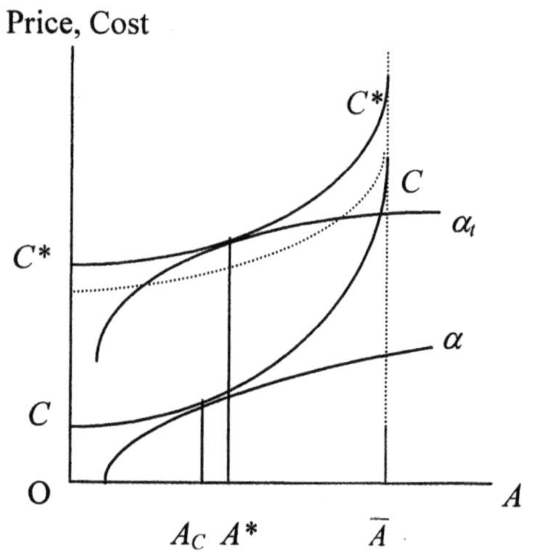

Figure 7.1: Ecological Dumping

But trade sanctions or taxes may not be complete solution to the above problem. A unit tariff imposed by the Northern government, which does not vary with the environmental-quality of Southern good, will simply protect the Northern producers without any impact on the quality of Southern good[23]. Only a pollution-content tariff, a tariff which varies (inversely) with the environmental-quality of the good, equivalent to the pollution-content production tax that is imposed on the Northern producers, can make Southern producers offer the socially optimum quality for exports to the Northern market. But this does not correct production distortions in the South fully because for the local market Southern producers still offer the cheaper sub-optimal quality. The same reasoning shows that an environmental standard imposed by the North, which requires A^* to be the minimum environmental-quality of imports, can only correct distortions associated with production for the Northern market. If maintaining dual qualities is not costly, the Southern producers will offer a lower environmental-quality of the good sold in the local market.

Moreover, both the pollution-content tariff and minimum environmental standard are sub-optimal policies for the North itself. As long as production pollution in the South does not spill over to the North, unlike the case of trans-boundary pollution, these policies are welfare reducing for the North compared to free trade. Northern consumers lose as they are forced to pay more for imports from the South than what they gain from having a higher environmental-quality, A^*, of such imports. The welfare loss is evident from Figure 7.1 as the Northern consumers, under imports restricted by a pollution-content tariff or environmental standard, are forced to move back to the higher indifference curve α_t. Thus achieving higher environmental-quality of imports through such trade policies cannot overcompensate the Northern consumers for the losses they suffer from the consequent increase in the price of imports.

In other words, improvement in the environment through better quality of the good may not necessarily make consumers and nations better off in terms of (net) welfare or surplus they derive from consuming such goods. This point is often overlooked and misunderstood in the discussion of trade sanctions against dirty exports of Southern countries. Such policies make sense for the Northern markets from a purely national welfare perspective, as we will show below, only in cases where production pollution in the

---

[23] See Sen and Acharyya (2002) for a more detailed discussion.

South has a trans-boundary character or when the environment is degraded not at the production stage but at the point of consumption.

Of course, one might argue and justify such restrictions on dirty imports from the South on grounds of protecting the global environment. But even in such cases of altruism, in which individuals in importing country are more concerned with environmental resources in the exporting country and do not mind paying more for such causes, trade taxes or regulations are not globally optimum as they cannot correct distortions fully even in the exporting country. In fact, the age-old theory of distortions, as developed by Bhagwati, Srinivasan, Haberler and Johnson, clearly tells us that only a production tax, or any combination of policies that has the same economic effects, is a first-best solution to a production externality. A production pollution being simply a case of production externality should also therefore be corrected through a (pollution-content) production tax. A trade tax and even an environmental regulation on imports are sub-optimal policies. These policies may, in fact, not even been second-best policy.

More effective policy option for the North, though once again not the first best one either from the Northern or global welfare perspective, is prohibiting Southern exports if Southern producers do not use a *cleaner* technology. A cleaner technology is privately costly, but lowers the environmental damage inflicted upon by the good. Thus, the social cost associated with such a technology is much smaller than that associated with a dirty technology as shown by the (broken) curve in Figure 7.1 lying below C^*C^*. If the marginal cost of improving the environmental-quality with this cleaner technology is the same as the (social) marginal cost associated with the old (dirtier) technology, then strict enforcement of cleaner technology improves the environment-quality of the Southern good exported to the Northern market to the same level as does the pollution-content tariff. For the North this is still a Pareto-inferior policy to free imports from purely welfare perspective.

For the South, on the other hand, such a trade sanction is at least better than the pollution-content tariff imposed by the North because it lowers the social cost associated with production for the Northern market. In absence of strict enforcement of environmental standards by the Southern government, producers there can still maintain a dual technology – the dirtier technology for local production and the cleaner technology for export production – but the social cost itself being lower for the cleaner technology, the Southern and global environment improves.

7.3 Consumption Pollution and Northern Regulations

As we have argued above, neither the case of national production pollution nor the concern for global environment (and welfare) can fully justify Northern trade restrictions or environmental regulations on dirty exports by the South. The same set of policies, however, make sense from purely Northern welfare perspective once we shift our focus from production pollution to the case of consumption pollution. Examples of environmental damages through consumption and the related issue of a negative consumption externality are overwhelming. Cigarette smoking, auto-emissions and use of non-recyclable bottles and packaging materials are only a few such cases. Catalytic converters in the automobiles and the rules regarding recycling of packaging materials, particularly the world-wide ban on the use of certain types of polythene packets, are a few measures that aim at reducing such negative consumption externalities.

But even in such cases, the use of environmental standards against the export of dirty varieties by the South is not a self-enforcing proposition because consumption pollution calls for a consumption tax as an optimal intervention. The issue is, therefore, whether an environmental standard or a pollution content tariff is Pareto-superior to free trade for the North. Moreover, if so, should the Northern government set the same standard for imports as it sets for its local producers?

To some extent, these issues have been addressed in Krutilla (1991), Ulph (1992) and Fischer and Serra (2000). Krutilla compared an optimal consumption (production) tax with a Pigouvian tax when the regulatory country is a net exporter and when it is a net importer of the good generating the negative consumption (production) externality. Ulph, on the other hand, examined the choice between environmental standards and taxes as policy instruments of the two national governments who use these instruments strategically to their respective national advantages. With production as the source of pollution, he showed that countries will prefer to use standards rather than taxes for *the same level of pollution*. This, however, falls short of an analysis that compares *optimal* policies. In a more recent paper, Fischer and Serra (2000) derive conditions under which the environmental standards are protectionist. In their duopoly model, there is a strategic (or rent-extracting) incentive for the use of environmental standards. Consequently, a social planner in the importing country raises the environmental standard when the foreign firm exports, which is higher than what would have been imposed if both the firms were domestic firms.

A somewhat different approach is adopted here drawing heavily from Acharyya (2000). When all the consumers care for higher environmental-quality of the good and the price they pay for it, the environmental-quality of the good itself is a choice variable for the producers. Moreover, since heterogeneous set of consumers have different preferences for such qualities, goods of different environmental-qualities are offered to different groups of consumers not only at the profit-maximizing competitive equilibrium but also at socially optimum equilibrium. Under such circumstances, if the Southern producers have genuine cost advantage compared to Northern producers in producing goods of lower environmental qualities, a uniform minimum standard imposed by the Northern government *may* be Pareto-superior to free trade provided the cost advantage of the South is not significant in the sense defined below. But even then, as shown below, a uniform standard on Southern exports of dirty varieties is just a second-best policy and, more importantly, such a second-best standard is *lower* than what might have been in force in the North before trade liberalization. This result is in sharp contrast to the result of Fischer and Serra (2000) where it is optimal to raise the standard in the importing country after trade opens up.

7.3.1 Environmental Quality in North under Autarchy

Consider a simple extension of the willingness-to-pay framework discussed in section 7.2. Suppose there are two types of Northern consumers who have different valuations for environmental-quality of the good they consume. Their type is parameterized by the variable α_j: High-type is denoted by α_H and the low-type by α_L ($\alpha_H > \alpha_L$). Each consumer buys, if at all, only one unit of the good. By this assumption we rule out any congestion effect which is of course for analytical convenience. No consumer is income constrained in the sense defined earlier in Chapter 3. Total demand for the good is, therefore, zero (when none buys the good), n_j (when only type-j consumers buy) or $n_L + n_H$ (when all buy the good).

Suppose, consumers can judge the environmental quality of the good (i.e., the degree of the environmental damage it causes) *before* they actually consume the good. Otherwise there would arise the problem of informational externality such as in the markets for lemons. Of course, consumers might still fail to fully internalize the social cost of consuming the good and consequently we have the standard consumption externality problem where private and social willingness to pay differs.

Under these assumptions, the purchase decision of consumers -- whether to buy and, if so, then what environmental-quality to select from amongst the available ones in the market – is governed by the same set of individual rationality and self-selection constraints like those specified in Chapter 3:

$$u(\alpha_j, A_j) \geq p_j \tag{7.2}$$

$$u(\alpha_j, A_j) - p_j \geq u(\alpha_i, A_i) - p_i \tag{7.3}$$

where $(A_j\ ,\ p_j)$ is the pair of environmental-quality and price targeted for type-j consumers.

Cost of production is convex in environmental quality but linear in the quantity of the good produced and sold:

$$C = c^N(A)x\ ,\ \ c_A^N(A) > 0,\ \ c_{AA}^N(A) > 0 \tag{7.4}$$

Of course we also assume $c_A^N(\overline{A}) > u_A(\alpha_H, \overline{A})$ to ensure interior solutions as explained earlier.

The unregulated competitive equilibrium in this Northern market under autarchy is illustrated in Figure 7.2. The quality levels, A_{HC} and A_{LC}, which correspond to tangency points e_H and e_L respectively along the (unit) cost curve, are offered to the high-type and the low-type consumers by the Northern competitive producers. The corresponding welfare levels (or private benefits) attained by the Northern consumers are indicated by the indifference curves $l l'$ and $h h'$ for the representative consumers.

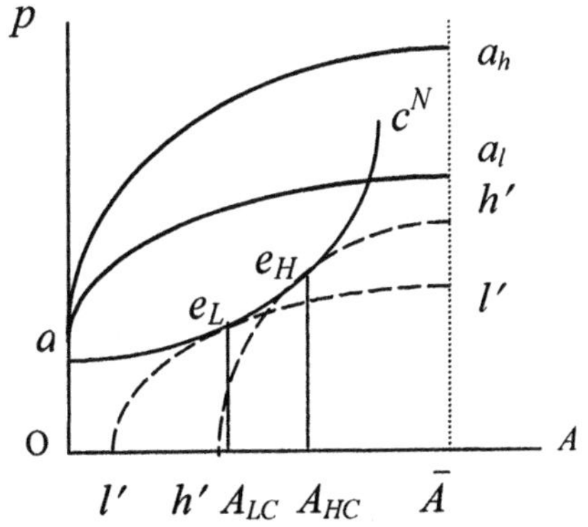

Figure 7.2: Competitive Environmental Qualities under Autarky

Formally, the sum of these autarkic private gains, denoted by B^a, equals,

$$B^a = \sum_{j=H,L} n_j[u(\alpha_j, A_{jC}) - c^N(A_{jC})] \tag{7.5}$$

But these competitive environmental quality levels are not the socially optimal qualities since the consumers do not internalize the social cost associated with the consumption pollution that the good generates. Thus, the private and the social valuations of the good differ. This has no conflict with our earlier assumption that consumers correctly perceive the environmental quality of the good by which we mean that there is no misperception about the private benefit from consuming the good. Since there is no a priori reason to believe why the high-income Northern consumers will internalize the social cost partially or fully even though they may have entirely different valuation of the private benefit they derive, we can expect similar divergence between social and private benefits from (or willingness-to-pay for) the good at the high-end of the market as well. Formally, if β denotes the social cost per unit due to the consumption pollution that is not internalized by the consumers, the following specification seems reasonable:

$$\beta = \beta(A), \ \beta_A(A) < 0, \ \beta_{AA}(A) < 0 \tag{7.6}$$

Therefore, the social welfare (or total surplus) realized from catering to the type-j consumers is,

$$W_j = n_j[u(\alpha_j, A) - c^N(A) - \beta(A)] \tag{7.7}$$

Let A_L^* and A_H^* be the socially optimum qualities offered to the two types. Figure 7.3 illustrates such an optimum quality A_H^* offered to the high type consumers. The curve $a_H^* a_H$ reflects the society's maximum willingness to pay for different environmental qualities. The marginal willingness to pay for a higher environmental quality for the social planner is greater than that of the high-type consumers. This means, if competitive producers would face consumers who would be willing to pay the social value, they would have raised the environmental quality of their good. Therefore, the socially optimum quality is greater than the competitive quality: $A_j^* > A_{iC}$, $j = H, L$. However, we assume that differences in social and private marginal willingness-to-pay is not so large as to lower A_{HC} even below A_L^*.

It is immediate that such socially optimum environmental qualities can be induced in a private economy through a policy which makes private benefits equal to the social benefit. In the present context of consumption distortion (pollution), an environmental quality-dependent or pollution-content consumption tax at the rate $t = \beta(A)$ achieves that and, therefore, is the first-best policy. But, since different types of consumers buy goods of different environmental qualities and inflict upon the society different degrees of consumption pollution, the tax rates applicable on them should also be different at the social optimum.

If, instead of such (type-specific) pollution-content consumption tax, a physical restriction such as a minimum environmental standard is imposed on the Northern producers, will it be Pareto-optimal? The answer is affirmative only if we can construct the optimal pollution-content consumption-tax equivalent environmental standards. Since the socially optimum environmental qualities in the two sub-markets are different, this requires discriminatory or non-uniform minimum environmental standards in the two sub-markets. In particular, by setting A_L^* as the standard in the low-end of the market and A_H^* as the standard in the high-end of the market, the Northern government can attain the Pareto-optimum situation.

But a uniform minimum environmental standard is what we typically observe in most of the countries imposing such standards since, the WTO

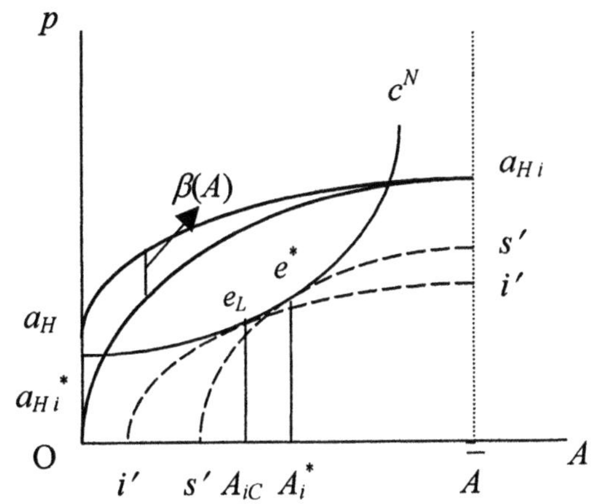

Figure 7.3: Sub-optimality of Competitive Environmental Quality for Type-H

requires standards based on the products rather than on the processes. Such requirements here can be interpreted as a uniform standard imposed on this quality-differentiated good. Thus it would be more relevant to compare a uniform standard with the Pareto-optimum consumption tax. Unfortunately, no such uniform standard exists which can be the first-best policy[24].

Under such circumstances, it is relevant to know which of the two consumption-tax equivalent environmental standards, A_L^* and A_H^*, is the second-best. This depends on the distribution of consumers over different types, as captured here by the relative size of the two types of consumers. In particular, as shown in the appendix, when the first-best consumption-tax equivalent discriminatory environmental standards cannot be set, setting the smaller of the two (i.e., A_L^*) as the minimum standard for the Northern producers is the second-best if,

$$\frac{n_L}{n_H} > \frac{[u(\alpha_H, A_H^*) - c^N(A_H^*) - \beta(A_H^*)] - [u(\alpha_H, A_{HC}) - c^N(A_{HC}) - \beta(A_{HC})]}{[u(\alpha_L, A_L^*) - c^N(A_L^*) - \beta(A_L^*)] - [u(\alpha_L, A_H^*) - c^N(A_H^*) - \beta(A_H^*)]} \tag{7.8}$$

When A_L^* is set as the minimum standard, the net private benefit for the low-type consumers falls because $A_{LC} < A_L^*$ is their optimum choice. If $A_L^* < A_{HC}$, the high-type consumers can still purchase their preferred variety A_{HC}, and therefore derive the same (net) benefit as when there is no such minimum standard imposed by the Northern government. But when $A_H^* > A_{HC}$ is set as the minimum environmental quality of the product, the benefit falls compared to the unregulated case for both types of consumers. Moreover, since the private benefit for the low-income consumers falls further because A_H^* takes them further away from their preferred variety and therefore puts them on an even higher indifference curve (and hence on a lower iso-net utility curve) than does A_L^*, the regime of higher minimum standard (A_H^*) unambiguously lowers the private benefit compared to the regime of lower minimum standard (A_L^*). But a higher environmental quality reduces the social cost, on the other hand, thereby raising the social welfare. If the low-type consumers are larger in number than a critical value, the loss in private benefit from setting a higher standard outweighs the gain in terms of a lower environmental pollution.

[24] See appendix for a formal proof.

Accordingly, the social welfare falls. This is precisely what has been stated in (7.8).

To summarize, under autarky, pollution content consumption tax or its equivalent discriminatory environmental standard is Pareto-optimal. A uniform minimum standard is only a second-best policy for the North. The distribution pattern, however, determines which of the two tax-equivalent standards would be the second-best.

7.3.2 Trade Liberalization in the North

Suppose the North liberalizes its trade regime allowing Southern firms to sell the good in the North. To isolate the issue of ecological dumping from regulation of Southern exports of dirty goods to the North, we assume that Southern firms have genuine cost advantage in dirty varieties. More precisely, consider the similar convex technology in the South as in the North with following properties:

$$c^S(0) < c^N(0) \tag{7.9a}$$

$$c^S(\hat{A}) = c^N(\hat{A}) \tag{7.9b}$$

$$c_A^S(A) > c_A^N(A) \quad \forall \; A \tag{7.9c}$$

where $A_{LC} < \hat{A} < A_{HC}$.

Thus what we assume is that though the marginal cost of quality enhancement is higher in the South than in the North (as specified in (7.9c)), which reflects among others a superior Northern technology, plant-specific (fixed) costs that are not related to quality of the product is lower in the South (as specified in (7.9a))[25]. The assumption made in (7.9b), on the other hand, specifies the comparative advantage of Southern (Northern) producers in lower (higher) quality varieties of the good. This means, as we will see, after trade opens up, there will effectively be a segmentation of the Northern market between Southern exporters and local Northern firms.

---

[25] An example of such quality independent cost per unit is the wage to the unskilled workers who perform the lower stages of activities in the production process.

Consider first the choices of the Northern and the Southern firms in the unregulated free trade scenario. That is, in what follows, we assume that initially no environmental standard was imposed on the Southern firms and trade was free. We shall later explore the welfare implications of the situation where initially there is the second-best standard, A_L^*, and the Southern firms are allowed to export their good to the North only when they meet such a product standard.

Despite the comparative advantage of Northern producers in the sense specified in (7.9b), if Southern producers' advantage in basic stages of production is too large, the Southern firms out compete the Northern firms in both the sub-markets in the North. In such a case, *all* Northern consumers buy imported varieties even though the locally available qualities may be superior. Let A_{jS} denotes the quality of the j-th imported variety. By (7.9c) and the marginal condition for selection of environmental qualities, $u_A(\alpha_j, A) = c_A^i(A)$, $i = N, S$, it is immediate that both the Southern qualities selected for the Northern market will be lower than those offered by the Northern producers. Since the consumption of imported lower qualities entails a loss of private benefit for the Northern consumers, the price of imports must be sufficiently low to over-compensate for this to induce all consumers to buy imported varieties. For competitive imports from the South, this means that Southern unit cost must be sufficiently lower than the Northern unit cost. From our specification of cost functions it is understandable that this will be the case when the Southern cost advantage is such that $A_{HS} < \hat{A}$[26]. Otherwise, the Northern firms cater to the high-income Northern consumers with the "autarkic" quality A_{HC} and the Southern firms cater to the low-income Northern consumers with a "lower" environmental quality, A_{LS}.

These equilibria are illustrated in Figure 7.4. The cost curve c^S corresponds to the case where Southern firms' cost advantage for $A < \hat{A} < A_{HC}$ is very large. Under autarky the high-type Northern consumers attained the net utility level hh' by purchasing the locally available higher environmental quality A_{HC}. When trade is liberalized in North, since c^S lies wholly above hh', the (net) utility level they can enjoy from purchasing the Southern good of quality A_{HS}, is strictly lower than what they get from purchasing the Northern good. But when the Southern cost curve is c_o^S, the high-

[26] More precisely, from the self-selection constraint of the high-type Northern consumers, it can be checked that for $A_{HS} < \hat{A} < A_{HC}$, southern cost must be such that $c^S(A_{HS}) \le c^N(A_{HC}) - u(\alpha_H, A_{HC}) + u(\alpha_H, A_{HS})$.

income Northern consumers enjoys a higher net utility from buying the Southern good, and consequently the Southern firms capture the high end of the Northern market as well.

As a simplification, and to avoid multiplicity of cases, we assume throughout the rest of our analysis that the Southern (absolute) cost advantage is significant so that both the Northern and the Southern firms operate in the North but at the two segmented ends of the market in the North.

Under this assumed market segmentation under free trade, the Northern welfare under equals,

$$W_T = n_L[u(\alpha_L, A_{LS}) - c^S(A_{LS}) - \beta(A_{LS})]$$
$$+ n_H[u(\alpha_H, A_{HC}) - c^N(A_{HC}) - \beta(A_{HC})] \qquad (7.10)$$

For the low-type Northern consumers, there are private gains, whereas the high-type consumers do not experience any welfare gain as they continue to consume the Northern good of the same environmental quality as they were under autarchy. The total private gain, therefore, is higher under free imports from the South. Still free trade is sub-optimal because of consumption externalities. However, this sub-optimal level of social gain

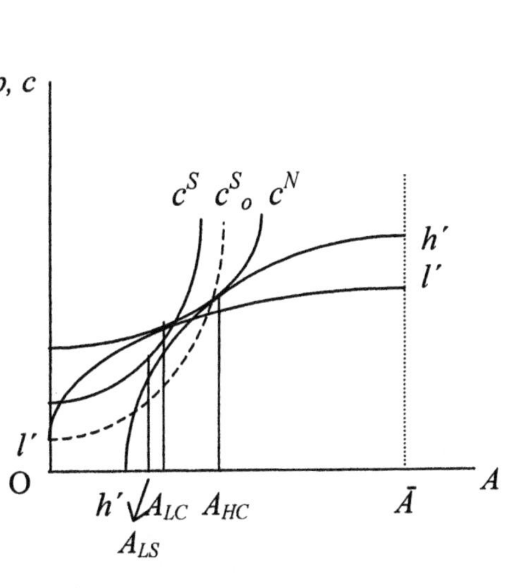

Figure 7.4: Southern Export of Dirty Variety

from free-trade is the benchmark level against which we need to weigh the welfare levels under environmental regulations and pollution-content tariffs to examine rationale for such policies apart from protecting the environment in the North.

7.3.3 Welfare Implications of Environmental Standards

First of all, note that free trade with pollution content consumption tax defined earlier is the first-best policy. This follows from the rule of optimal intervention in presence of externalities [Johnson (1965)]. What we must look at, therefore, is whether the environmental standard which is a second-best under autarky is still so. In a sense, we examine whether the environmental-standard restricted trade (ESRT) is Pareto-superior to free trade. We, however, limit our attention to the income distribution pattern defined in (7.8) and thus consider A_L^* as the reference minimum environmental standard (ES).

Before considering the welfare implication of trade with such a minimum environmental standard imposed on Southern exports to North, note that any environmental standard, $\tilde{A}$, prohibits all trade if this standard is higher than the critical environmental quality $\hat{A}$ as defined in (7.9b). For export of such a minimum standard, the Southern firms charge the low-type Northern consumers a price equal to the corresponding unit cost (of production), $c^S(\tilde{A})$. The Northern producers, on the other hand, charge a price equal to their marginal cost for the same variety, $c^N(\tilde{A})$. But, since by (7.9b), $c^S(\tilde{A}) > c^N(\tilde{A})$ for $\tilde{A} > \hat{A}$, all low-type Northern consumers buy the low-priced Northern good. Hence, all imports from South are effectively prohibited by any minimum environmental standard $\tilde{A}$ greater than $\hat{A}$.

But when the minimum environmental standard $\tilde{A}$ set by the Northern government is lower than $\hat{A}$, the Southern firms can sell their good at a lower price than the Northern producers and consequently trade takes place. We label all such non-prohibitive minimum environmental standards as the regime of environmental-standard restricted trade (ESRT) in rest of the analysis.

We are now in a position to examine welfare implications of setting the autarkic (second-best) environmental quality A_L^* as the minimum environmental standards for Southern exports. It is immediate from the above discussion that if $A_L^* > \hat{A}$, such a standard on Southern exports will be prohibitively high and therefore the same social welfare level will attained in the North as under autarky (with the same minimum environmental standard). More precisely, denoting the social welfare attained by the North under a prohibitive minimum environmental standards for imports from South by W_{PES}, we can write it as,

$$W_{PES} = n_L[u(\alpha_L, A_L^*) - c^N(A_L^*) - \beta(A_L^*)]$$
$$+ n_H[u(\alpha_H, A_{HC}) - c^N(A_{HC}) - \beta(A_{HC})] \qquad (7.11a)$$

But if such a minimum standard is non-prohibitive, the Southern firms can cater to the low-income Northern consumers and the Northern welfare under such ESRT will equal,

$$W_{ESRT} = n_L[u(\alpha_L, A_L^*) - c^S(A_L^*) - \beta(A_L^*)]$$
$$+ n_H[u(\alpha_H, A_{HC}) - c^N(A_{HC}) - \beta(A_{HC})] \qquad (7.11b)$$

The social welfare (per capita) under the prohibitive environmental standard in the lower segment of the Northern market is indicated in Figure 7.5 by the curve labeled $S_E S_E$ passing through the point E. This will be lower than the free trade welfare level if the Southern cost advantage is such that the free trade equilibrium for low-income consumers occurs at a point like e_S (along the Southern cost curve) below $S_E S_E$. Otherwise, for the Southern cost curve passing through the segment AB, the prohibitive environmental standard will be Pareto-superior to free trade.

Formally, by the assumed nature of the post-trade equilibrium, we have to compare the welfare level in the lower segment of the Northern market under free trade with that under the prohibitive environmental standard. These are the first terms in the right hand side of (7.10) and (7.11a) respectively. Hence, free trade is Pareto-superior to the prohibitive environmental standard if the Southern cost advantage is such that:

$$c^S(A_{LS}) < c^N(A_L^*) - [\beta(A_{LS}) - \beta(A_L^*)] - [u(\alpha_L, A_L^*) - u(\alpha_L, A_{LS}) \qquad (7.12)$$

Thus, if the pre-trade (second-best) environmental standard is prohibitive, it is Pareto-inferior to free trade for the North when the Southern firms have significant cost advantage satisfying (7.12).

This result highlights the gains from free trade for the North. A prohibitive environmental standard raises the social welfare in North by prohibiting the low-type Northern consumers from buying the low-quality Southern imports and consequently reducing the consumption pollution. But at the same time it robs off the opportunity of having the low-price imports from the South that reflects its cost advantage in producing the lower quality varieties. If Southern firms have significant cost advantage over the Northern firms, the gain from the low-price imports from the South under free trade is more than the gain from smaller consumption pollution under the prohibitive environmental standard, causing the free trade Pareto-superior to the prohibitive environmental standard.

But, when the pre-trade second-best environmental standard is not prohibitive, Pareto-superiority of free trade depends no longer on the Southern cost advantage. Instead, the curvature property of the Southern cost function relative to that of the utility function of the low-income Northern consumers, and the damage or social cost function, $\beta(A)$, are important. This is immediate by comparing the first terms in the right hand sides of (7.10) and (7.11b). The reason behind such a difference in the conditions for Pareto-superiority of free trade in the two cases is simple. A prohibitive environmental standard causes a switch from imports from the cost-efficient Southern firms (under free trade) to the inefficient Northern production.

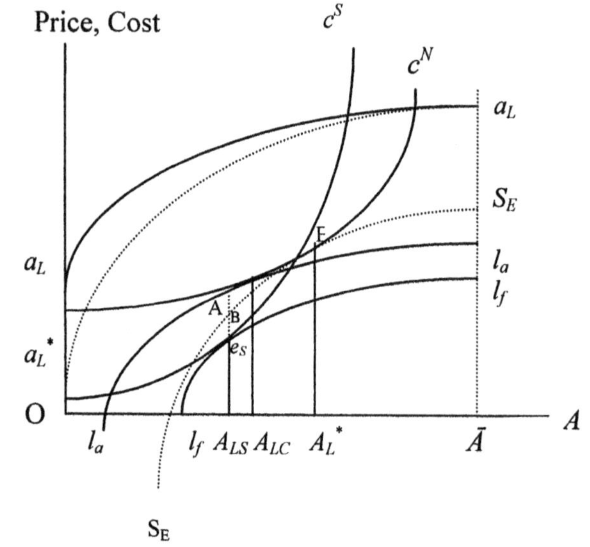

Figure 7.5: Prohibitive Environmental Standard vs. Free Trade

Thus, the extent of the cost advantage of the Southern firms is the key factor. But a non-prohibitive environmental standard, instead of causing such a switch to the Northern producers, raises the cost of exports for the Southern producers and accordingly forces them to raise the price. Thus, it is the rate of change in such costs that now determines the welfare ranking of the free trade and the non-prohibitive environmental standard. However, it may be more convenient to express the condition for Pareto-superiority of the free trade to the non-prohibitive environmental standard (i.e., to ESRT) in terms of the private and the social benefits:

$$\beta(A_{LS})-\beta(A_L^*)<[u(\alpha_L,A_{LS})-c^S(A_{LS})]-[u(\alpha_L,A_L^*)-c^S(A_L^*)] \qquad (7.13)$$

Note that the right hand side captures the loss of private benefit from the ESRT as the environmental standard forces the low-type Northern consumers to buy their sub-optimal variety, whereas the left hand side measures the social gain due to smaller consumption pollution. What follows, therefore, is that, the ESRT, with the (non-prohibitive) pre-trade standard is Pareto-inferior to free trade for the North when the social gain from a lower pollution level is sufficiently small.

The conditional statements made in the last two results imply that depending on the parametric values of the model, an environmental standard, whether prohibitive or non-prohibitive, may be desirable to free trade for the North. This result is to be distinguished from that of Fischer and Serra (2000). First of all, an environmental standard need not be protective to improve the Northern welfare. The non-prohibitive environmental standard does not at all protect the Northern producers catering to the low-income Northern consumers, and yet may be welfare improving. Second, such a welfare improving ESRT does not necessitate any strategic or rent-extracting effect as in Fischer and Serra (2000).

So far our discussion of ESRT (and prohibitive environmental standard) has been based on the pre-trade (second-best) environmental standard, A_L^*. Should the Northern government maintain this as the minimum standard for imports when trade opens up? Or should the minimum environmental standard be lowered as the South has a comparative advantage in dirtier varieties? The answer depends on whether the pre-trade environmental standard is still the second-best standard in the post trade scenario. First of all, if conditions (7.12) and (7.13) hold, then such an environmental standard is of course not the second-best policy for the North. On the other hand, if this standard is Pareto-superior to free trade, by the assumed distribution pattern in (7.8), it will be a second-best policy for the North.

On the other hand, if this standard is Pareto-superior to free trade, by the assumed distribution pattern in (7.8), it will be a second-best policy in the post trade scenario only if it is the smaller of the pair of environmental qualities consistent with the first-best consumption tax under free trade. Just as under autarky, the (non-uniform) first-best environmental standards under free trade would be those corresponding to optimal consumption taxes. Setting the smaller of those environmental qualities as a uniform standard would be the second-best policy for the North under the same distribution pattern as specified in (7.18). But as shown in the appendix, under free imports from the South, the optimal environmental quality induced by the first-best consumption tax on the low-income Northern consumers is $A_L^*{}_S$ which is lower than, A_L^*.

Thus, if $A_L^*{}_S$ is set as the minimum environmental standard by the North for both local goods as well as imports from the South when trade opens up, it will be Pareto-superior to the autarkic second-best standard, A_L^*. In other words, the ESRT with a minimum standard $A_L^*{}_S$ lower than the autarchic standard, A_L^*, on the Southern goods is the second-best policy for the North. This result holds regardless of the extent of the Southern cost advantage (as defined in (7.12)) and whether the autarkic environmental standard is prohibitive or not.

Therefore, when the South has genuine comparative cost advantage in producing dirtier varieties, imposing the same standard on such imports from the South as was imposed on Northern producers under autarky will clearly be welfare reducing for the North. When first-best consumption taxes are not implemented in the North, the minimum standard on imports from South should be lowered from the autarkic (second-best) level. But, if the environmental regulation imposed by the North is targeted to induce the South to export the same quality as the Northern firms were offering before trade liberalization, this is certainly welfare reducing for the North.

The reason is simple. When the Northern government sets the higher (autarkic) environmental standard for Southern exporters, individual and aggregate welfare increase since the marginal utility is strictly positive. But a higher environmental quality can be provided only at a higher price to cover additional costs. Since cost increases faster than the gain in utility for any environmental quality greater than the socially optimum level,

$A_L^*{}_S$, the additional price paid by the Northern consumers is more than the additional gain from the higher environmental quality set by the environmental standard in the North. In other words, the loss associated with a lowering of the environmental standard from A_L^* to $A_L^*{}_S$, is more than compensated by the lower price of the Southern good under competitive conditions. Thus, social welfare increases when the minimum standard is lowered from the autarkic level. Note that, since the consumption tax merely redistributes income from the Northern consumers to the Northern government, the gain in welfare for the Northern consumers under physical regulation due to zero tax burden is exactly matched by the corresponding revenue loss for the government.

7.4 Environmental Regulation and Employment in the South

So far our discussions have been focused on optimality of environmental taxes and regulations from the Northern and global welfare perspectives. Apart from such welfare considerations, the impact these policies may have on employment opportunities in the South is not to be undermined. In fact, political resistance to implementation of environmental taxes and regulations in the South has often been grounded on the perceived adverse employment effect. Since the cleaner varieties are usually relatively capital intensive, change in the production pattern towards these goods and, therefore, reallocation of labour across different sectors, as a consequence of stringent standards, are likely to cause a significant proportion of the workforce to become unemployed. With employment in the formal sectors dwindling in size in most of the Southern countries due to forces of globalization and trade liberalization, further displacement of workers as a consequence of higher environmental standards is hard to negotiate politically.

To illustrate, consider a simple extension of the above analysis to the three-sector framework of a small open economy discussed in Chapters 4 and 5. With a little reinterpretation of the three goods – the differentiated (export) good Z and homogeneous composite traded good T and non-traded good N – such a general equilibrium framework would be a convenient framework for analyzing this issue. Suppose, good Z is the one with environmental implications, and just as specified above, the environmental damage that this good causes diminishes as its (environmental) quality improves. If foreign consumers care for the environment and are aware of different environmental-qualities in which good Z can be made available, their willingness-to-pay will vary positively with such a quality: $P_Z^{*\prime}(A) > 0$. The composite traded good and the non-traded good, on the other hand, have no environmental impact whatsoever, and are thus assumed to be available in only one variety. The production structure is the same as specified earlier. For any given environmental-quality of good Z, skilled labour and physical capital are combined in fixed proportions per unit of production of good Z. But cleaner varieties of good Z, i.e., varieties with higher environmental-quality (A), require more intensive use of physical capital per unit of output. The other goods are produced by unskilled labour and physical labour, once again in fixed proportions.

Replicating the argument for selection of the quality of good Z, we can reproduce Figure 4.1 as Figure 7.6 to illustrate the competitive environmental-quality that will prevail in our small unregulated open economy denoted by A_C, for any given set of factor prices. But the major difference with the earlier analysis is that now we have externalities arising as a consequence of private agents not internalizing the environmental damages that this good causes while consuming or producing the good.

Suppose, the good Z degrades the environment when it is consumed. Since we assume that the good is not locally consumed but its entire production is for the export market, the negative consumption externality arises abroad. This is shown by the differences between the private willingness-to-pay schedule $P_Z^*(A)$, labeled PP, and the social willingness-to-pay schedule abroad, labeled ss. The optimal environmental quality for the North is A^* which once again can be achieved through a consumption tax. Alternatively, an environmental regulation requiring A^* as the minimum standard forces all producers to offer the optimal quality.

To examine what employment implications these policies may have for the South, consider an initial less-than-full-employment equilibrium as an outcome of a rigid money wage for the unskilled workers which is set above the market-clearing level in the South. For a given world price of the composite traded good, a higher money wage must lower the rate of return to capital to make production of this good viable in the South. If the non-traded good is relatively labour (capital) intensive, its average cost of production and therefore price rise (fall) despite fall in the capital cost. This in turn lowers (raises) the demand for non-traded good causing reallocation of resources away from the labour-intensive non-traded (composite traded) good. Aggregate employment of unskilled labour therefore falls below its total supply.

Given such an initial situation of unemployment of unskilled workers in the South, an environmental regulation in the North requiring enhancement of the environmental quality of Southern exports to the level A^*, raises the demand for capital in the export sector because higher environmental quality is more intensive in physical capital. With the Southern capital stock fully engaged in production initially, production of higher environmental quality to meet the Northern standard is possible only through withdrawal of some capital that were previously engaged in production of the composite traded good and the non-traded good.

Such reduction in the availability of capital stock for the rest-of-the-economy in the South, comprising the composite traded and non-traded sectors, must changes the production levels. Note that since the environmental regulation does not affect the world price of the composite traded good, the rate of return to capital does not change given the rigid unskilled money wage. This means the price of the non-traded good does not change either, and accordingly for any given real income, the economy will consume the same amount of the non-traded good as before. Since the (domestic) market for this good must clear locally, the production of non-traded good must, therefore, be at the same level as it was corresponding to the unregulated competitive environmental quality of the export good, A_C. That is, withdrawal of capital from rest-of-the-economy to sustain production of higher environmental-quality of the export good lowers *only* the production of the composite traded good regardless of any factor intensity conditions. Aggregate employment of unskilled labour thus falls unambiguously as a consequence of an environmental regulation.

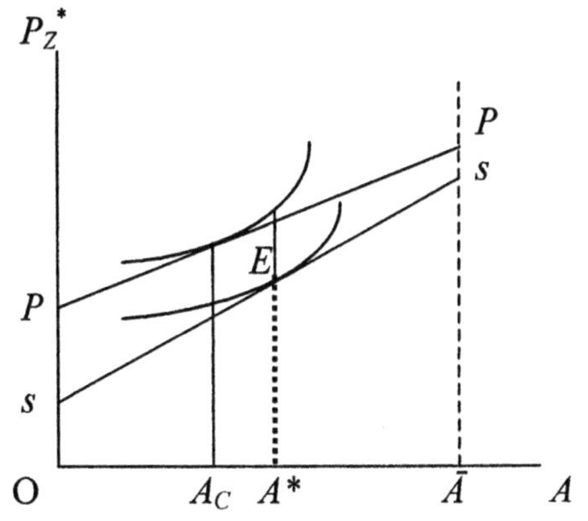

Figure 7.6: Competitive Environmental Quality and Global Optimum

In fact, employment will fall even further due to real income effect. Note that, since the rate of return to capital cannot adjust as its value is tied down by the world price of the composite traded good and the rigid unskilled money wage, even though the skilled money wage falls to make the production of good Z viable (at point E on PP in Figure 7.5), the marginal condition for Southern producers of good Z is violated at the minimum environmental quality A^*:

$$a'_{KZ}(A^*)r > P_Z^{*'}(A^*) \tag{7.14}$$

The environmental regulation thus generates a production distortion in the South and lowers the real income there. This in turn lowers the demand for both the non-traded and the composite traded goods. Aggregate production and therefore demand for unskilled labour falls further reinforcing the adverse supply effect (or output-composition effect) of the environmental regulation.

The above analysis formalizes the general apprehension in the South that an environmental regulation will cause greater unemployment of unskilled workers. But such regulations may also have a favourable effect on productivity and employment of workers[27]. The productivity gain from spatial separation of dirty and clean industries through international trade, and its welfare implication for the trading countries has been formalized by Copeland and Taylor (1999). Sen and Acharyya (2002), on the other hand, demonstrate how such external effects of an environmental standard may create scope for an employment expansion. The essence of the argument can once again be illustrated in terms of the above three-sector framework.

However, since good Z is not consumed domestically, for higher environmental-quality of the good to have any positive impact on health situation of workers and therefore on their productivity, we now must assume that environmental damages are caused when the good is produced.

Consider Figure 7.7 which illustrates output levels of the composite traded good and the non-traded good and the level of employment of unskilled workers. The $K^*(A_C)$ curve gives us the different combinations of these

[27] There is some evidence of improvement in labour productivity in the lead-smelting sector in India as a consequence of improvement of health that higher environmental standards in production has brought in [Chakrabarti and Mitra (2000)].

two goods that the South can at most produce using up all its domestic capital which is available after production of the export good Z, $\overline{K}$ - $a_{KZ}(A_C)Z$. Recall from the basic assumption of the benchmark model developed in Chapter 4 that the output of the export good Z is fixed by the availability of skilled labour, specific in production of this good, and the fixed input-output ratio in which this it is used in production: $Z = \overline{S}/a_{SZ}$. Thus, capital availability for production of other goods varies inversely with the environmental quality of the export good.

To keep things simple, suppose the environmental quality of the export good affects productivity of unskilled labour only and that such productivity effects are the same for all workers regardless of whether they work in the composite traded sector or in the non-traded sector. The broken flatter line is the locus of output combinations that the South could produce if all unskilled workers were fully employed. But, as explained above, suppose initially due to higher rigid unskilled money wage, the price of non-traded good (which is relatively labour intensive in Figure 7.6) is too high, and therefore its demand is too low, to generate employment for all unskilled workers. The line passing through point E and parallel to the L-line indicates the aggregate employment corresponding to the unregulated competitive environmental quality A_C of the export good.

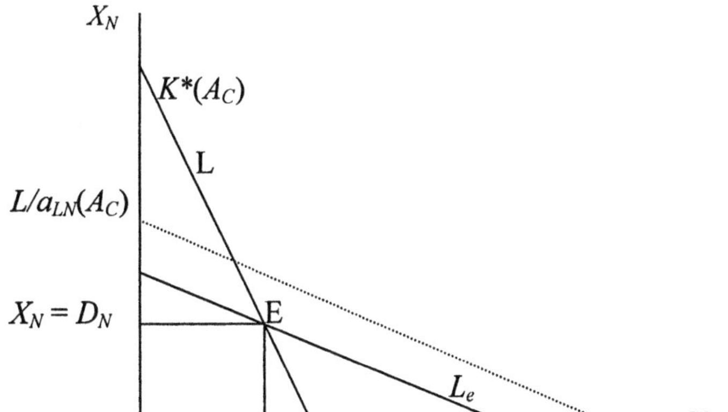

Figure 7.7: Environmental Regulation, Productivity Gain and Aggregate Employment

An environmental regulation that forces the Southern exporters to raise the environmental quality now triggers three effects. First is the supply effect as spelled out above: The availability of capital for these sectors falls which at the initial price of the non-traded good, lowers the production of the composite traded good. Thus, aggregate employment falls on this account.

Second, as the productivity of all unskilled workers improves, the effective labour supply increases in the economy. That is, the same levels of output now can be produced by less number of workers. Notationally, a_{LT} and a_{LN} decline as the environmental quality improves. On this account, unemployment rises too at initial output combinations at point E. In Figure 7.6, the L-line shifts out and thereby increases the gap between the aggregate employment line and the L-line which measures the level of unemployment.

The third effect that environmental regulation generates is the price effect which raises aggregate employment of unskilled workers. The productivity improvement lowers the labour cost all around at the rigid money wage. In the composite traded sector, the lower labour cost benefits the capital owners by raising the rate of return to capital. A little manipulation of the zero-profit condition in the composite traded sector (see eq. (4.9)) shows this:

$$\hat{r} = -\frac{\theta_{LT}}{\theta_{KT}}\hat{a}_{LT} \tag{7.15}$$

If the non-traded good is relatively labour intensive, its price falls which in turn raises its demand. Production of non-traded good thus rises and that of the composite traded good falls.

If the non-traded good is relatively capital intensive, on the other hand, increased capital cost hits this sector more than labour-productivity improvement saves upon the labour cost. Its price increases as a consequence, which lowers its demand and therefore production. In both cases, composition of output moves in favour of the relatively labour-intensive good, for any given (net) capital stock available for production of these goods. Aggregate employment thus increases by this demand-led output changes.

What emerges from all these discussions are that, under the possibility of a productivity improvement, no longer the contractionary implications of an environmental regulation is a foregone conclusion. Aggregate employment of unskilled workers falls only if the price elasticity of demand for non-traded good is sufficiently small. Otherwise, the favourable demand effect raises aggregate employment by outweighing the adverse supply effects.

7.5 Conclusion

In public as well as academic debates, ecological dumping by Southern countries and their genuine comparative advantage in dirty goods or varieties are often not distinguished from each other. Consequently the standard gains from North-South trade are overlooked. Once such (static) efficiency aspect is brought in, environmental regulations on Southern exports is no longer a first-best policy, globally as well as for the North. Such regulations on trade thus appear as new faces of non-tariff barriers to protect the Northern producers from competitive imports from the South.

Appendix

I. Sub-optimality of Uniform Minimum Environmental Standard

Let us begin with A_L^* set as the minimum uniform standard by the Northern government. The Northern producers thus must choose environmental qualities from the set $[A_L^*, \overline{A}]$. Let $A_L^E \in [A_L^*, \overline{A}]$ be the environmental quality offered the low-type Northern consumers. Thus the benefit they derive equals,

$$B_L^E = n_L[u(\alpha_L, A_L^E) - c^N(A_L^E)] \qquad \text{(A.7.1)}$$

whereas the social benefit from such an environmental quality equals,

$$W_L^E = n_L[u(\alpha_L, A_L^E) - c^N(A_L^E) - \beta(A_L^E)] \qquad \text{(A.7.2)}$$

But by competitive forces, at equilibrium, all producers catering to the low-type Northern consumers will offer the minimum environmental standard, A_L^*. If any firm offers a higher quality, it will have zero demand.

This is because, since A_L^* is greater than the unregulated competitive quality A_{LC}, by the curvature properties it is immediate that,

$$u(\alpha_L, A) - c^N(A) < u(\alpha_L, A_L^*) - c^N(A_L^*) \quad \forall A > A_L^*$$

That is, under marginal-cost pricing, low-type consumers derive strictly lower net utility by purchasing any quality higher than the minimum environmental-quality, and therefore, will prefer A_L^* to any such quality. This means, the social welfare generated in the low-end of the market under such a minimum standard will exactly equal to what can be achieved through a Pareto-optimal consumption tax on low-type consumers.

But if $A_L^* < A_{HC}$, the high-type consumers will be offered this unregulated competitive quality which is sub-optimal. On the other hand, if $A_L^* > A_{HC}$, producers will offer them A_L^*, because for the same reason as spelled out above, any producer offering a higher quality to the high-type consumers will have zero demand. Since $A_L^* < A_H^*$, once again this is sub-optimal. Therefore, setting A_L^* as the *uniform* minimum environmental standard for all variety of goods regardless of for whom such varieties are targeted, is not a first-best policy.

Similar logic shows that setting A_H^* as the *uniform* minimum environmental standard is not a first-best policy. On the other hand, it is needless to check, though easy to understand, that setting any environmental quality other than these two as *uniform* minimum environmental standard cannot also be first-best. In fact, social welfare will in such cases be even lower than what can be attained for A_L^* or A_H^* as the minimum standard.

II. Second-best (Uniform) Standard under Autarchy

As argued above, when A_L^* is set as the uniform minimum standard, the producers will choose the quality A_L^* for the low-type consumers and A_H^* for the high-type consumers if $A_L^* < A_{HC}$. But if A_H^* is set as the minimum standard, then *all* consumers are offered this quality. Social welfare attained in these cases then equal,

$$W^E(A_L^*) = n_L[u(\alpha_L, A_L^*) - c^N(A_L^*) - \beta(A_L^*)]$$
$$+ n_H[u(\alpha_H, A_{HC}) - c^N(A_{HC}) - \beta(A_{HC})]$$

$$W^E(A_H^*) = \sum_{j=L}^{H} n_j [u(\alpha_j, A_H^*) - c^N(A_H^*) - \beta(A_H^*)]$$

It is then straightforward to check that $W^E(A_L^*) > W^E(A_H^*)$ if the distribution pattern satisfies (7.8) in the text.

III. Second-best (Uniform) Standard on Imports from South

It is sufficient to show that when Southern firms have a cost advantage that allows them to cater to the Northern consumers and such imports are not prohibited by the Northern government, the optimal quality under the first-best consumption tax, $A_{L}^{*}{}_{S}$, is lower than the optimal quality under autarchy, A_L^*.

Note that, $A_{L}^{*}{}_{S}$ and A_L^* are such that,

$$u_A(\alpha_L, A_{LS}^*) = c_A^S(A_{LS}^*) + \beta_A(A_{LS}^*) \tag{A.7.3}$$

$$u_A(\alpha_L, A_L^*) = c_A^N(A_L^*) + \beta_A(A_L^*) \tag{A.7.4}$$

Now suppose on the contrary that $A_{L}^{*}{}_{S} \geq A_L^*$. Since marginal utility is diminishing in environmental quality, by (A.7.3) and (A.7.4) this presumption implies,

$$c_A^S(A_{LS}^*) - c_A^N(A_L^*) \leq \beta_A(A_L^*) - \beta_A(A_{LS}^*) \tag{A.7.5}$$

On the other hand, since (negative) social marginal cost is lower for higher environmental quality, so the right-hand-side of (A.7.5) must be non-positive. Hence,

$$c_A^S(A_{LS}^*) < c_A^N(A_L^*) \tag{A.7.6}$$

But this contradicts the assumption that Southern firms have higher marginal cost of quality than Northern firms which means, if $A_{L}^{*}{}_{S} \geq A_L^*$,

$$c_A^S(A_{LS}^*) > c_A^S(A_L^*) > c_A^N(A_L^*)$$

Hence $A_L^{*}{}_S < A_L^{*}$.

That is, when Southern firms have cost advantages, the optimal quality under the first-best consumption tax, $A_L^{*}{}_S$, is lower than the optimal quality under autarchy, A_L^{*}.

List of Figures

List of Tables

Bibliography

Acharyya, R. (1995): Liberalization, Innovation and Exports. The Economic and Political Weekly, Vol. XXX.

Acharyya, R. (1998): Monopoly and Product Quality: Separating or Pooling Menu? Economics Letters 61, 187-94.

Acharyya, R. (2001): Purchasing Power Constraint, Income Disparities and Vertical Product Differentiation. In: A. Guha, K.L. Krishna and A. Lahiri (Eds.): Industry and Trade: Essays by NIPFP-Ford Foundation Fellows. Vikas Publishing House, New Delhi.

Acharyya, R. (2000): Southern Exports of Dirty Variety and Optimality of Environmental Standards: Case of Consumption Pollution. Working Paper # 2, DSA Centre for Studies in Regional Economics, Department of Economics, Jadavpur University.

Acharyya, R. (2005): Quality Discrimination among Income Constrained Consumers. Forthcoming in Economics Letters.

Acharyya, R. (2005): Consumer Targeting under Quality Competition in a Liberalized Vertically Differentiated Market. Journal of Economic Development 30(1).

Acharyya, R., and S. Bandyopadhyay (2004): Process and Product Innovation: Complementarity. Japanese Economic Review 55 (2), 175 – 200.

Acharyya, R., and S. Bandyopadhyay (2004): Does Input Sector Liberalization Promote Quality Innovation and Exports? Forthcoming in International Review of Economics and Finance.

Acharyya, R., and R. W. Jones (2001): Export quality and Income Distribution in a Small Open Economy. International Review of Economics and Finance 10, 337-351.

Acharyya, R., and A. Raychaudhuri (2001): Indo-EU Trade Relations. UGC Minor Research Project Report, Jadavpur University.

Acharyya, R., and A. Raychaudhuri (2005): Non-Price Factors, Comparative Advantage and Trade Performance. The Indian Experience. In: R. Acharyya (Ed.): Essays on International Trade. Theory and Policy for the Developing Economies. Allied Publishers Private Limited.

Acharyya, R., and P. Roy Chowdhury (2004): Innovation incentives in an integrated market with vertical product differentiation. Paper presented at the conference on 75 Years of Development Research at the Cornell University during May 7-9.

Akerlof, G. (1970): The Market for Lemons. Quarterly Journal of Economics LXXXIV, 488-500.

Allen, F. (1984): Reputation and Product Quality. Rand Journal of Economics, Autumn, 311-327.

Armington, P. S. (1969): A Theory of Demand for Products Distinguished by Place of Production. IMF Staff Papers 16, 159-178.

Balassa, B. (1979): The Changing Pattern of Comparative Advantage in Manufactured Goods. The Review of Economics and Statistics 61, 259-66.

Basu, I. (2001): A Study of India's Software Export Performance in the Nineties. Unpublished M.Phil Dissertation. Jadavpur University, Calcutta.

Becker, G. (1965): A Theory of the Allocation of Time. Economic Journal 55, 493-517.

Besanko, D., Donnenfeld, S., and L. J. White (1988): The Multiproduct Firm, Quality Choice and Regulation. Journal of Industrial Economics 36, 411-30.

Bhagwati, J.N., and T. N. Srinivasan (1963): Domestic Distortions and the Theory of Optimum Subsidy. Journal of Political Economy, February.

Chakrabarti, S. and N. Mitra (2000): A Report on Cost Benefit Analysis of Air Pollution Control Technology. A Case Study of Secondary Lead Smelting Industries. West Bengal Pollution Control Board.

Chiang, S.C., and R. Masson (1988): Domestic Industrial Structure and Export Upgrading: A Quality Signaling Approach. International Economic Review 29, 261-270.

Clemenz, G. (1990): International R&D Competition and Trade Policy. Journal of International Economics 28, 93-113.

Cooper, R. (1984): On Allocative Distortions in Problems of Self-selection. Rand Journal of Economics 15, 569-77.

Copeland, B., and A. Kotwal (1996): Product Quality and the Theory of Comparative Advantage. European Economic Review 40, 1745-1760.

Copeland, B., and S. Taylor (1994): North-South Trade and Environment. Quarterly Journal of Economics, August, 755-87.

Copeland, B., and S. Taylor (1995): Trade and Transboundary Pollution. The American Economic Review 85, 716-737.

Copeland, B., and S. Taylor (1999): Trade, Spatial Separation and the Environment. Journal of International Economics 47, 137 - 68.

Darby, M. R., and E. Karni (1973): Free Competition and the Optimal Amount of Fraud. Journal of Law and Economics 16, 67-88.

Dasgupta, S., Mody, A., Roy, S., and D. Wheeler (2001): Environmental Regulation and Development: A Cross-Country Empirical Analysis. Oxford Development Studies 29(2), 173-187.

Dean, J. (1992): Trade and Environment: A Survey of Literature. In: P. Low (Ed.): International Trade and Environment, World Bank Discussion Paper No. 159.

Donnenfeld, S., and W. Mayer (1987): The Quality of Export Products and Optimal Trade Policy. International Economic Review 28, 159-174.

Donnenfeld, S. and S. Weber (1987): The Quality of Export Products and Optimal Trade Policy. International Economic Review, February.

Esfahani, H.S. (1991): Reputation and Uncertainty: Towards an Explanation of Quality Problems in Competitive LDC Markets. Journal of

Development Economics 35, 1-32.

Falvey, R., and H. Kierzkowski (1987): Product Quality, Intra-industry Trade and (Im)perfect Competition. In: H. Kierzkowski (Ed.): Protection and Competition in International Trade, Basil Blackwell.

Findlay, R., and H. Kierzkowski (1983): International Trade and Human Capital: A Simple General Equilibrium Model. Journal of Political Economy 91, 957-978.

Fischer, R., and P. Serra (2000): Standards and Protection. Journal of International Economics 52, 377 - 400.

Flam, H., and E. Helpman (1987): Vertical Product Differentiation and North-South Trade. American Economic Review 77, 810-822.

Gabszweicz, J.J., and J. F. Thisse (1979): Price Competition, Quality and Income Disparities. Journal of Economic Theory 20, 340-59.

Gabszewicz, J., and X. Wauthy (2002): Quality Underprovision by a Monopolist When Quality is Not Costly. Economics Letters 77(1), 65-72.

Gruen, F.H., and W.M. Corden (1970): A Tariff that Worsens the Terms of Trade. In: I.A. McDougall and R.H. Snape (Eds.): Studies in International Economics. North Holland: Amsterdam.

Heeks, R. (1996): India's Software Industry. Sage Publication: New Delhi.

Johnson, H.G. (1965): Optimal Trade Intervention in Presence of Domestic Distortions. In: R. E. Baldwin et. al. (Eds.): Trade, Growth and Balance of Payments: Essays in Honour of G. Haberler. North Holland, Amsterdam.

Jones, R. W. (1965): The Structure of Simple General Equilibrium Models. Journal of Political Economy 73, 557-72.

Jones, R.W., H. Beladi and S. Marjit (1999): The Three Faces of Factor Intensities. Journal of International Economics 48(2), 413-20.

Kim, J-H, and J-C Kim (1996): Quality Choice of a Multiproduct Monopolist and Spill-over Effect. Economics Letters 52, 345-52.

Klein, B. and K.B. Leffler (1981): The Role of Market Forces in Assuring Contractual Performance. Journal of Political Economy 89, 615-41.

Krutilla, K. (1991): Environmental Regulation in an Open Economy. Journal of Environmental Economics and Management 20, 127-42.

Laffont, J-J., and J. Tirole (1993): A Theory of Incentives in Procurement and Regulation. MIT Press, Cambridge, MA.

Lall, S. (1984): India's Technological Capacity: Effects of Trade, Industrial, Science and Technology Policies. In: M. Fransman and K. King (Eds.): Technological Capability in the Third World. Macmillan, London.

Lall, S. (2001): The Technological Structure and Performance of Developing Country Manufactured Exports, 1985-1998. Oxford Development Studies 28(3).

Levinson, A. (1996): Environmental Regulation and Manufacturers Location Choices: Evidence from the Census of Manufacturers. Journal of Public Economics 62, 5-29.

Low, P., and A. Yeats (1992): Do 'Dirty' Industries Migrate? In: Low, P. (Ed.): International Trade and the Environment. World Bank Discussion Paper No. 159.

Marjit, S. (2000): Economic Reform and Informalization in a Developing Economy: A General Equilibrium Analysis. DSA Working Paper 15/2000, Jawaharlal Nehru University.

Marjit, S. (2003): Economic Reform and Informal Wage: A General Equilibrium Analysis. Journal of Development Economics 72, 371-78.

Marjit, S., and A. Raychaudhuri (1997): India's Exports: An analytical Study. Oxford University Press, New Delhi.

Murphy, K.V., and A. Shleifer (1997): Quality and Trade. Journal of Development Economics 53, 1-15.

Mussa, M., and S. Rosen (1978): Monopoly and Product Quality. Journal of Economic Theory 18, 301-17.

Nelson, P. (1974): Advertising as Information. Journal of Political Economy (July/August), 729-54.

Oxfam International (2002): Rigged Rules and Double Standards: Trade, Globalization and the Fight against Poverty. Oxfam International Advocacy Office, Washington.

Rashid, S. (1988): Quality in Contestable Markets. Quarterly Journal of Economics, February, 245-249.

Rauscher, M. (1994): On Ecological Dumping. Oxford Economic Papers 46, 822-840.

Raychaudhuri, A., R. Acharyya, S. Marjit, M. Rahman and M. Tipu (2003): Trade Potentials of the South Asian Economies Under the New Global Trade Regime. The Role of Some Non-Price Factors: A Case Study of India, Bangladesh and Sri Lanka. SANEI-IV Project Report.

Reitzes, J.D. (1991): The Impact of Quotas and Tariffs on Strategic R&D Behaviour. International Economic Review 32 (4), 985-1007.

Rodrik, D. (1992): Closing the Productivity Gap: Does Trade Liberalization Really Help? In: G.K. Helleiner (Ed.): Trade Policy, Industrialization and Development: New Perspectives. Oxford, Clarendon Press.

Sanyal, K., and R. Acharyya (2001): Environmental Issues in a Globalized World: An Overview. In: Acharyya, R., and B. Moitra (Eds.): Effects of Globalization on Industry and Environment. Lancers Books, New Delhi.

Sen, A., and R. Acharyya (2002): Environmental Regulation and Employment: Does a Trade-off Exist? Paper presented at the Annual Conference on Models and Methods In Economics at the Indian Statistical Institute, Calcutta in January 2002. Working Paper # 5/2001, DSA Centre, Department of Economics, Jadavpur University.

Sen, A., and R. Acharyya (2002): Pollution Content Tariff, Environmental Quality and Welfare. In: R. Khasnobis (Ed.): Issues in Sustainable Development. University of Calcutta Press, Calcutta.

Shaked, A., and J. Sutton (1982): Relaxing Price Competition through

Product Differentiation. Review of Economic Studies 49, 3-13.

Shapiro, C. (1983): Premiums for High Quality Products as Returns to Reputation. Quarterly Journal of Economics, 659-679.

Sharma, A., G. Faber and P.K. Mehta (1997): Meeting the Challenges of the European Union. Sage, New Delhi.

Srinagesh, P. and R.M. Bradburd (1989): Quality Distortion by a Discriminating Monopolist. The American Economic Review 79, 96-105.

Srinivasan, T.N. and J.N. Bhagwati (1995): Trade and Environment: Does environmental diversity detract from the case for free trade? Working Paper No. 721, Economic Growth Centre, Yale University.

Tirole, J. (1989): The Theory of Industrial Organization. MIT Press, Cambridge.

Tobey, J. (1990): The Effects of Domestic Environmental Policies on Patterns of World Trade: An Empirical Test. Kyklos 43(2), 191-209.

Ulph, A. (1992): The Choice of Environmental Policy Instruments and Strategic International Trade. In: R. Pethig (Ed.): Conflicts and Cooperation in Managing Environmental Resources.

White, L.J. (1977): Market Structure and Product Variety. American Economic Review 67, 179-82.

Wilson, J.S., T. Otsuki and M. Sewadeh (2002): Dirty Exports and Environmental Regulation: Do Standards Matter? Working Paper, Development Research Group, World Bank.

Index

GPSR Compliance

The European Union's (EU) General Product Safety Regulation (GPSR) is a set of rules that requires consumer products to be safe and our obligations to ensure this.

If you have any concerns about our products, you can contact us on ProductSafety@springernature.com

In case Publisher is established outside the EU, the EU authorized representative is:

Springer Nature Customer Service Center GmbH
Europaplatz 3
69115 Heidelberg, Germany

Batch number: 10725973

Printed by Printforce, the Netherlands